INSTANT ACTING

Published by Betterway Books, an imprint of F&W Publications, Inc., 1507 Dana Avenue, Cincinnati, Ohio, 45207. First edition.

98 97 96 95 94 5 4 3 2 1

Library of Congress Cataloging in Publication Data

Whelan, Jeremy
Instant acting / by Jeremy Whelan – 1st ed.
p. cm.
Includes index.
ISBN 1-55870-370-5
1. Acting. 2. Audiotapes. I. Title.
PN2061.W476 1994
792'.028 – dc20 94-16271
CIP

Designed by Leslie Meaux-Druley
Cover photograph by Sandy Underwood: Bruce Longworth in Cincinnati Playhouse in the Park's production of *Our Country's Good*

DEDICATION

This book is dedicated to my parents,
John and Mary, and to my sister and brothers,
Patrica, Michael and John, and their families.

It is also dedicated to my daughter L.A. and her family.

ACKNOWLEDGMENTS

Thanks to Steve Neal, of Barry University in Miami Shores, and his wonderful *Steel Magnolias* cast. Thanks also to Professor Frank Olly from St. Josephs University in Philadelphia; Robert Christope of the University of the Arts in Philadelphia; Professor Robert Yowell, Chair of Theater, California State University; Mel and Barbara Shrawder, formerly of the University of Miami. Gracias a mi former student Maritza Sanabia for getting the Spanish translation of *The ABC's of Acting* off to such a fine start, and also for being a friend. Merci, Severine Ziegler for doing the same in the French translation of *The ABC's of Acting*. Thanks to former student Greg Stott for help along the way. A special thanks to the crew at Copymat, especially Wayne Williams, whose help on the computer was absolutely vital and to Louie Zelaya, Claudio Mota, and Benny Behrooz. Thanks to Renee Soucee for being a friend. To Valmar Oleska. Thank you, Michael Whelan, for some invaluable editorial advise. Photographer Nathaneal Welsh for the photos. To John Brent and Jo Forsberg for being an important part of my education as an actor.

ABOUT THE AUTHOR

Jeremy Whelan has been an acting professional for the past thirty years, starring in productions from feature films to TV commercials to off-Broadway theater. He is the author of *The ABC's of Acting* (Grey Heron Books). Whelan frequently conducts acting workshops and seminars.

TABLE OF CONTENTS

PREFACE

Eight years and thousands of hours working with hundreds of professional and student actors went into creating and refining the rehearsal and acting technique described in this book.

Whether you are an actor or director/teacher, this technique breaks down many of the walls that exist between those two roles. Certain sections of this book address the actor, others address the director, and some make no distinction. This book presents a brand-new approach to acting and a completely different way of looking at the actor-director relationship. Breaking with tradition is difficult, but in this case it inspires immense creativity.

Whatever your job—actor, director or teacher—I urge you to read the whole book. The technique presented here requires that actors and directors adjust their approach. In a way, this book is a script to better acting, but the roles of actor and director have been changed. These are not stock characters; the relationship is more complex.

The first time you try the Tape Technique described in chapter one, you'll feel liberated. Mastering the subtleties of that technique and learning how and when to use the other techniques in this book will take some time. Since being an actor is what you are and not what you do, you have the time. I am going to take you step by step through the technique, with a first and second rehearsal as examples and a checklist of do's and don'ts.

There will be many temptations to break the rules I have set up, but resist at first. I have spent many years working with this technique and thousands of trials and errors are behind me. You may well improve upon my ideas or even discount some of them. What remains will add an exciting, creative dimension to your acting, directing and teaching for the rest of your life. Enjoy it!

You obviously found your way into the acting section of that bookstore or library for a reason: You wanted to learn how to be a better actor, director or teacher. If you're just starting out, you're lucky. Not all have the same gifts—some will never be better than average; others will show genius. Some will offer their best as actors, some as directors, and some as teachers. Whatever you have to offer, you're going to find it faster within this book. If you've been in the game, it will be tougher on you. Progress always changes some of the rules, so it's back to school for you. However, the rewards are plentiful and they come quickly.

There are eighteen ways to implement this low-tech, high-impact tecnique. You will hopefully try them all at some point, and may find others. They free the actor—professional or beginner—in a way superior to any other technique I know.

Welcome to *Instant Acting*.

Jeremy Whelan,
November 11, 1993

INTRODUCTION

Instant Acting describes and relies heavily on an acting and rehearsal technique I refer to as the Whelan Tape Technique. Simply put, the technique is this: You read your lines into a tape recorder, and then you put your script down and act out the scene to the playback of the taped lines.

The technique is simple to use once you know the rules. At first the rules will seem numerous, but most of them are common sense once you see what the technique does for you. If kids had to learn all the rules of baseball before they were allowed to play, the game would be dead before they started. "I'll throw the ball and you try to hit it with the bat." That's the way most of us got started with baseball. We thought it was fun so we learned the rest.

If I took that fun approach with the Whelan Tape Technique, I would tell you, "Take a three-page scene and read it into a tape recorder. Then as you play it back, act it out. Don't move your lips. It's emotional surfing. Ride it." When you're done, tape the scene again, and act it out again to the new recording. Do that five times. Then get into your first emotion and do the scene—no tape, no script. Take a minute, and when you're ready, say the first line. The rest should fall out of your mouth and show up in your movements.

Some of you might put down this book and give the technique a shot right now. Go ahead—be fearless, have fun. Then come back. As you learn the rest of the rules, the technique requires more creativity and becomes much more fun. You might want more information before you begin, so read a few more pages until you get the idea. Please remember that I've spent thousands of hours refining this technique, so do come back to the book to discover more insight and advice.

The main reason this technique works so well was noted by an actress in Florida. After her first run-through using the technique, she said, "That's the first time I actually heard everything the other actors were saying. With my script in hand, I was using so much energy just in the mechanics of reading—holding the script, and trying to find where I was and where they were—that I never really heard what they were saying. This way I heard every word. It was great. I could really feel it."

Using the Tape Technique, you will quickly notice certain advantages that I will briefly point out now and describe later in detail. To help you remember the key elements, use the mnemonic "COMPT," which represents "free theatre":

C = Contact with the material and with other actors is constant, which stimulates emotional penetration of characters and relationships.

O = Organic blocking is discovered by the characters. They are moved physically by the emotional stimulus of the lines.

M = Memorization of lines is automatic as a natural result of the above.

P = Prevention of premature vocal characterization (which always happens when reading from a script prevents contact among actors).

T = True to the script. The actors should always use the exact words of the script. It's not important if the script is pure poetry or it cost a million dollars; the professional actor's first obligation is to the text.

Your sole obligation when using the Whelan Tape Technique is to listen, to really hear, to discover the emotional truth of the line and let it move you. The famous choreographer George Balanchine said that in classical dance, movement begets emotion. In modern dance, emotion begets movement. In acting, the feelings that move us often come out in words, but the words are only the bowl in which the soup is served.

Remember what I said about baseball. Don't try to learn all the rules before you start to play with this idea. Just read them over once and get a sense of what you're doing, then get on your feet and give it a try. When you come back to the rules, you'll find that many will have become obvious while working the technique. There is a very strong logic underlying this technique, so following one rule will trigger many others.

SECTION ONE

THE WHELAN TAPE TECHNIQUE FOR BETTER ACTING

Chapter One

Introducing the Whelan Tape Technique

To begin using the Whelan Tape Technique, take a tape recorder and any number of actors involved in any script. Sit them around a table and have them read the script to get a sense of it. They must be exposed to all of the major given circumstances of their individual characters, such as missing a foot, anorexia or a French accent. Then they read the script again, only this time audiotaping the read. Immediately, the actors get up, and act out the scene—without moving their lips—to the playback of the tape. The script should immediately be experienced emotionally, physically and intellectually. This technique integrates many aspects of character that traditionally were broken into little pieces and then put back together later. That method succeeded in spite of itself and only because actors worked so hard. This new technique develops the emotional, physical and intellectual traits all at once.

From here on I'll be doing a very detailed step-by-step guide. It may be too detailed for some. Go through it my way this first time, and then play with it any way you want. I do not follow this format all the time, but it will be useful for you to get many of the major points at once. This example outlines a first rehearsal with two actors doing a three- to four-page scene, working for about two hours. For more information on how to choose a scene, see chapter seven. For warm-up exercises, see chapter six.

It's time for the first taping for run-through.

Basic Rules for the Whelan Tape Technique:

1. *Black out stage directions from your script.* That was the past, another director, another actor. It's your part now; do it your way.

2. *Put the tape recorder close enough to both actors to make a clean recording*—one that can be heard from any part of the playing area. If you are in a theater that has a house system, use that.

3. *Do a sound check.* Record three or four lines, and then play the tape back to make sure you're recording. Technical mess-ups happen, and too much time gets wasted when you go through the whole script, only to find that you weren't recording. Sound check every time you tape.

4. *Do only one take.* If you mess up a line, don't worry about it. Keep going. If you stop to fix a line, your partner will also demand a second take, and you'll waste a great deal of time on performance—something you should not be concerned about right now. This is first day, first time, one take, that's the rule.

5. *Don't rush the reading.* The natural tendency of an actor approaching a new script is to rush it. If you walk past an audition, and you see an actor beating his head against the wall, walk up to him and say, "You rushed it, didn't you?" (Nine out of ten times you'll be right.)

6. *Stay on the script.* Read every word just the way it's written. Stay on the script; don't try to make eye contact. By the way, if there's an unfamiliar word in the script, look it up. You should never say a word unless you know what it means.

7. *Don't try to act.* Don't force anything or deny anything. Just read the script and let it happen.

8. *Never use the same taping twice.* Always use a fresh taping for each run-through, because whether you realize it or not, you have grown during the previous run-through. You can't wear the same shoes you wore when you were five.

THE FIRST RUN-THROUGH

After you've taped the scene, you're ready for your first run-through. Before playing the tape, make some attempt to at least "fake" a set and some props. Three chairs can be a wall, a plant can be a forest or a garden and a stick can be a gun.

Central to this stage is keeping in mind that there are three basic moves an actor can make, and they are in response to the emotional content of the line. In acting, the emotional content of the line will move you:

1. Away From—**Repelled**
2. Toward—**Impelled**
3. To Remain—**Compelled**

I will go into more detail about these movements later.

Basic Rules for the Run-Through

Don't try to memorize the following rules for a run-through. Just read them and let them sink in.

1. *Don't perform.* You are not to consider what you are doing as being important to anyone, except yourself and the other actor. Don't force anything. Don't deny anything, but don't work for anything. Discount performance 100 percent.

2. *Don't move your lips.* You kill it. Instead of being a character in the moment, you're an actor worrying about lip synching. This is so important, and it gives actors a great deal of trouble when they first encounter the technique. What you must understand is that the whole point of the technique is to have you fully focused on your character and your relationship to the other characters at that moment. Sometimes actors move their lips without knowing it—a sure sign they are not in character. They are in their

heads, as an actor. They are not only out of character, but they are in the past as an actor, trying to remember what they said so as to lip sync it in the future. How could anything honest or interesting happen when an actor is so far away from what is going on at the moment? Directors must watch for this and stop it quickly. If you're an actor working without a director and you see your partner's lips moving, consider that you're up there by yourself, and it makes no sense to continue. It's like playing tennis by yourself. You hit the ball, but there is nobody there to hit it back. Gently make the other actor aware of what is happening.

3. *Don't try to remember what you're going to say next.* Stay in the moment.

4. *Don't negate any impulse unless it makes the other actor bleed or walk funny.* Note: I would never want to do or say anything that would restrict an actor's spontaneity, but how far that goes is something the actors discuss before they start the work.

5. *Don't put any obligation on yourself, other than responding to the emotional stimulus of the script, from as much of the character that you have at this point.* When I say "from as much of the character as you have at this point," I mean, when an actor reads a script, she gets some immediate ideas about character. This has to happen, and it is all you have to start with, but be aware that that conception is superficial. It has to be—you've only had the character a short time. Once you start acting with the tape recorder, the contact with the other actors may change your character's emotions from the way you saw him while reading. In other words, the character you *read* may be very different from the character you *meet.*

Let go of your original intellectual impression, and go with what you feel at the exact moment you look at or touch that other actor. It's not as obvious or as easy as it sounds. Guard your concentration. Stay in the moment.

6. *Don't stop yourself from eating, drinking, smoking, sucking on a lollipop, or anything else that would normally keep you from talking.* During one of my Miami workshops, a student took a long drink of whiskey in character, while the tape was playing back his lines. I knew the scene was far enough along that the students could hit most of the dialogue, so I had them do the scene again

right away. Since they were running with dialogue, the actor, of course, could not drink as he had done during the tape-recorded scene. However, the tension of a man wanting a drink very badly was in the actor's eyes, hands, back, and feet. It had not been there before he had followed his impulse to drink while acting to the tape. The situation went from passive (not drinking) to active (energetically suppressing the desire to drink).

7. *Do maintain contact with your partner:* eyes, hands, feet, props (light a cigarette, pour a drink), set (look out the window, throw pebbles in the lake).

8. *Don't be literal in expressing the Repels-Impels-Compels.* Let them explode. Impulse is art. Follow it blindly in rehearsal, and discipline it in performance—but never negate it. Negating creative impulse takes so much energy that you will appear spastic.

What do I mean by nonliteral Repels-Impels-Compels? Let's say you're playing a shy guy who gets invited into the apartment of the woman of his dreams. All of a sudden you get the impulse to scream, bounce off the couch, and tackle her. Do it! The fact that the character's personality would only let him respond with a few halting steps in her direction, is what defines his character. If, however, you fulfill the impulse, physically and emotionally, letting it fill you completely, when later, the more dominant aspects of character start to control the "style" of the movement, the audience should see beyond those few halting steps in her direction. They will see the tension of the denied desire to bounce off the couch and tackle her.

9. *Focus on your emotions.* How do you feel saying that? How do you feel hearing that? Let the emotion move you. Repel-Impel-Compel.

10. *Guard your concentration.* With all this newfound freedom, you might get tempted to think about what you did instead of what you're feeling at the moment. Don't!

11. *Do make hand and body gestures, verbal sounds without speech.* Feel free to laugh, cry, grunt, stick your tongue out, flip the bird, point, whistle, or scream. But don't get so loud that you can't hear the dialogue clearly.

12. *Don't stop for any reason once you start the tape.* Stay in character until it's over.

Now, start the tape and dive in. Remember, follow all impulses blindly.

Between the First and Second Tapings

Whether you were acting or watching that first run-through, a few of the major advantages of this technique probably became obvious to you. For example:

C = Contact should be constant. Eye contact is possible all the way through the scene, play or film. Physical contact is increased because hands are free to caress, fight or handle props. This constant and total contact allows the emotional flow between characters to build constantly.

Every time actors use the Tape Technique, they make one or more major connections to the character during the first time through. They get a very strong Repel-Impel-Compel from character. Most important, don't analyze this connection to death. Just do it again.

Don't fall in love with the way you said something the first time. Don't fall in love with the way you did something the first time. Your character will grow every time you do this technique. Growth means change!

When you remember what you did or how you said something, it is because you don't believe you can do it any better. There are no limits to your creativity. Go deeper; there is better in you.

THE SECOND RUN-THROUGH

Tape the scene again and act to it as you play it back. Remember to be sensitive to the Repels-Impels-Compels. How do you feel when you say that? How do you feel when you hear that? Let the feeling move you any way it wants. It's like emotional surfing – ride it. Remember: Don't remember!

Between the Second and Third Tapings

Some of the emotions you got the first time you did the scene were stronger this second time, and you probably found some new emotions. After only two run-throughs with the Tape Technique, you can see that movement is increasing, and rudimentary blocking has begun. This leads to another advantage of the technique:

O = Organic Blocking is discovered by the characters as they respond to the emotional stimulus of the Repels-Impels-Compels. Remember that these basic moves are in response to the emotional content of the line. The emotion forces you away from (Repelled), toward (Impelled), or to remain (Compelled).

Repels-Impels-Compels move the actor naturally around the playing area. A roughed out set and some hand props create homes for these Repels-Impels-Compels. A bar down left, for example, might be the home for a Repel.

THE THIRD RUN-THROUGH

This is technically not a run-through, rather an exercise. Set yourselves up to perform a basic mirror exercise. A mirror exercise is simply this: You and another actor stand facing each other a few feet apart, and one person mimicks everything the other person does. Don't get tricky. Move in super slow motion. Never move so fast that you can't be comfortably followed. Feet alike, hands alike, eyes alike, and backs alike, bend, stretch, sit, and lie down, just like a mirror image. Use the whole body. Start the tape. When you hear your voice, you lead, and your partner mirrors you. When your partner speaks, he or she leads and you are the mirror. Follow the Repels-Impels-Compels, but don't break the mirror.

I first worked with mirror exercises in 1964 at a workshop using Viola Spolin's theater games at The Committee, a San Francisco improvisation group. I have always found them highly effective, and they adapt incredibly to the Tape Technique. I've gotten incredible results using this Tape Technique variation with a five-character ensemble piece.

Here are three mirror exercises you should use:

Mirror Exercise I

Set up a basic mirror exercise (as above) and do it while listening to the playback of the freshly taped scene. The character speaking is the person looking in the mirror or leading. The actors should work far enough from each other so they can respond to the Repels-Impels-Compels.

The movement can be literal or stylized. Most often, since all movements must be slow enough to be mirrored, this means stylized. The taping is at normal speed, but the movement usually is something like the slow-motion replays of professional sporting events. Within that framework, Repels-Impels-Compels can be profitably followed. A slow-motion punch can be thrown. Just remember you can't go through the mirror. An embrace can be mirrored, but remember it is a mirror image. You cannot touch beyond the ways you can touch a real mirror. Remember, if the tape is playing your voice, you are leading, but be ready to mirror when your partner starts to speak. As always, stay in character.

Many valuable discoveries are made doing this exercise. Repels-Impels-Compels that were missed in your initial contact with the material become obvious while doing Mirror Exercise I.

Mirror Exercise II

Tape the scene again. This time the person speaking is the follower. The speaker mirrors the reaction of whomever he is speaking to. Take the Repels-Impels-Compels as they present themselves. Remember to stylize the movement. Slow it down enough to be followed.

Mirror Exercise III

Retape the scene. This time there won't be a leader or a follower. Nobody will lead, and nobody will follow. You will give and take, and help each other. Don't always lead, or let yourself be led. Try to get in sync, flow with each other. At first, one will lead, and then the other will lead. It will go back and forth like that, but there will be a moment—and you won't remember where it started—when you are just flowing, and it is absolutely effortless. You will love it. The tape will play and the scene will go on. You will hear your character's voice, and the other person will answer you. The emotions will flow through you, and you will both be absolutely in sync.

Don't get disappointed if this doesn't happen right away; it will happen eventually. It sounds hard, but if you really try to synchronize with each other, it will happen, and the character discoveries will be very rich. You will be pleased and surprised by your success and insights.

You can do Mirror Exercises I, II and III as part of one rehearsal, or you can spread them out. Break them up with any variation you want. Just be sure to do them all at some point.

It's obvious that this technique locks the actors into the script. It is an advantage to all concerned that the technique has the actors:

T = True to the script – 100 percent. The actors always relate to the exact words of the script. It's not important if the script is pure poetry, or if it cost a million dollars. The professional actor's first obligation is to the text.

Being true to the script is, in a way, like placing a kid in a playpen. Once in the playpen the child is usually safe. If the actors are forced to stay on the script, they should be safe to explore whatever happens. To extend the analogy, put some toys in the playpen and the child is not only safe but also happy. By adding some props inside the area defined by the script, the actors should be able to creatively explore the total experience.

I love improvisation and find it a very useful rehearsal tool, but never inside the script. It is too easy for the actor to take off into subjective areas that undermine the integrity of the script. For example, an actor in a psycho-drama might play her own divorce instead of the character's.

I always have the actors improvise any relationship prior to the script. I also like to investigate any possible future relationship between the characters by improvising. But inside the script they must work with the lines.

THE FOURTH RUN-THROUGH

Now tape the scene again and run it on the set. Only this time, if you have a director, use the Whelan Pause Technique. That is, the director will occasionally pause the tape playback. If the director is not there, leave long pauses or beats between speeches when recording. Use that time to penetrate the emotion generated by what you just said or heard. The following is a thorough description of how to use the Pause Technique, first for directors and then for actors.

THE PAUSE TECHNIQUE FOR DIRECTORS

I believe this to be a most significant technique that produces some outstanding results. I find the Pause Technique works best after the actors have gone through the Whelan Tape Technique two or three times. The actors should not attempt the Pause Technique until the third or fourth time because they need the initial run-throughs to assimilate the broad outline of the piece and to get a feel for the emotional flow. Without the script to hide behind and be distracted by, the actors are thrown into a naked confrontation with some pretty overwhelming emotional circumstances. Prolonging those moments for unlimited amounts of time can be a little more gut-wrenching than some actors are ready for. Actors have been hiding behind scripts so long it's almost in their DNA.

So let them try the Tape Technique and get used to it. By the fourth time or so, you, the director, are aware of moments that are being missed, moments you want the actors to explore more. When those moments come up, press the pause button.

With the old script-in-hand technique, you would have had to talk to the actors about a "beat," maybe giving them more than you wanted to. Now all you have to do is hit the pause button and watch the actors tear themselves apart until they get it. They will love you for it.

As in all this work, patience is the key. Don't worry about time. You're saving so much time with this technique you can afford to be patient. Having read the script and run the tape a few times, the actors are now somewhat comfortable working this way. They know the rules:

1. Stay in character no matter what.
2. Stay in contact: eyes, hands, props, etc.
3. Follow the Repels-Impels-Compels.

If rule 1 is working, rules 2 and 3 will follow automatically.

Tell the actors that at certain points you are going to pause the tape. They are to get in touch with how they feel when they say or hear the last line. To go deeper into the emotion generated by that line. To penetrate that emotion with every fiber of their being. You may leave them there for a long time to make sure they don't lose their concentration. Never let them slip into mere "waiting." Actually you can see that happen. The tension goes. The posture changes. When that happens, side coach, "Feel it in your back. Feel that emotion in your toes. Does it make you want to move? Feel it in your butt. Go deeper into the emotion." Direction like that should get them back into it.

Note: How long you hold them is up to you, but I seldom go over three minutes on any one pause. Again, play with it. It's new work, an open door. I don't know what would happen if I left the actors there a half hour. They might make a whole dynamic play out of that one beat, melt the stage, quit the class. I don't know. The inventiveness here can be overwhelmingly creative. The business the actors invent, while dealing with this tension, is some of the most creative work I've ever seen.

Note: As a director, I would always pick these big juicy moments to have the actors pause. Once, however, I had to leave the room, so I had a student press the pause button. When I returned unnoticed, I waited at the back of the room to observe the situation. It turned out to be quite interesting. The student on the pause button was working some moments I would never have chosen. He was pausing on what had seemed to me minor beats, and the results were yielding some very rich moments. I suppose the point here is to look beyond those bombastic beats. There are little gems in scripts that get missed, but when added, they provide a lustrous setting for those big jewels in the crown. Maybe another point is to have somebody else pop the button now and then.

THE PAUSE TECHNIQUE FOR UNDIRECTED ACTORS

Actors working alone who still want to benefit from the Pause Technique have three ways to go. Whichever you use, you must be very focused and disciplined. Realistically, however, if you are paused for a long time, you could lose your concentration.

A director will notice when you lose concentration and guide you back with some gentle side-coaching. However, when you're on your own, be vigilant. If you catch yourself slipping, kick your own butt back into the scene. Get back to the emotion. As soon as you get in touch with that, your concentration will strengthen and the work will go the way it's supposed to.

Don't rush. Use the extra time to penetrate a lifetime of emotional and physical coordination.

That's fairly self-explanatory, but maybe it deserves a few words. Your character—no matter how old—has been conditioned by his or her circumstances to respond to various emotional stimuli in a certain manner. In other words, she has, over a lifetime, found her own unique way of physically expressing each emotion, and her way differs from yours.

Now that you know how the director should guide you, this is what I want you to do:

1. Agree with your partner that either one of you can press the pause button at any time.
2. Agree that whoever paused the tape must also start it again.
3. When you are taping, leave long pauses between speeches, or leave long beats within a speech.

Although this means that you know when the pause will end, you still have enough time to explore the emotion. Using any of the above techniques is certainly more beneficial than running the scene at a more normal speed.

You may find that major vocal changes occur after running the Pause Technique. You should notice significant changes in line readings as the emotional involvement grows with each run-through. This occurs because:

P = Prevents premature vocal characterization. Premature vocal characterization always happens when a script in hand prevents contact with other characters. The script is like a full-body Roman battle shield: Nothing gets in, and nothing gets out. So shielded, the actor first creates characterization intellectually, which comes out in the voice. Once the scripts are finally memorized and the actors can make contact, they are left with two choices:

1. The character discoveries, which always flow from direct

contact, are forcibly stuffed into the prematurely formed vocal characterization.

2. The actor wastes a great deal of energy trying to break out of that premature vocal characterization, which, in some instances, had weeks of script-in-hand rehearsal to reinforce its negative influence.

Between the Fourth and Fifth Run-Throughs

By now all sorts of interesting things are happening. Without ever trying to memorize the lines, you know most of them. But be careful with this! You must guard your concentration so you don't slip into the future. Don't anticipate a line or a piece of business. Your partner might deliver a line in a way you don't anticipate. The time it takes you to recover from your partner's spontaneity will kill any creativity that could have come out of that moment and all the moments before that when you were in the future anticipating the next moment. Guard your concentration. Stay deeply involved with the emotion that is coming from what you just heard or said. Stay in the moment!

After the Fifth Run-Through

By now you will have seen how the other advantages of the Tape Technique apply, but a very significant advantage should now come home with a bang. The actors do not know how much has gone in, but they know almost all the dialogue and much of the character by now. The technique integrates all these, which helps you:

M = memorize the lines automatically. After five or so tapings, the actors can memorize a short scene of three or four pages without consciously trying. This happens because the actors use all their memories:

PIE = **P**hysical memory
Intellectual memory
Emotional memory

In the rote memorization process, only the brain, or intellectual memory, is involved. This technique, in effect, adds two-thirds more memory. The effect is synergistic: The whole is equal to more than the sum of its parts. Learning is much quicker this way because the memories are working as a team.

THE SIXTH RUN-THROUGH

This is not an improv. Follow the script!

If you have a director, or a good actor to "do book" for you, or even if you're on your own, go ahead and try the scene without the tape recording. You probably will be somewhat insecure. Don't worry. You know more than you realize. Just say the first line, and the rest will pretty much follow. Don't panic and start calling for your line. Give yourself a chance. There is no performance aspect to rehearsal, so take your time. The lines come easier as you get deeper into the script and emotion. Here, as in the early stages of the Whelan Tape Technique, your only crime is breaking character before the scene is over. If you remember a section of the scene you forgot, say it was in the beginning, and you're in the middle, just throw your partner the cue line for that section. He will probably pick up the cue, and you will go right through. When you get back to the middle, just keep acting. Do that part over. Stay on the script. Don't start improvising. If you're lost, ask for your line.

You will probably find that you remember 60 to 90 percent of the dialogue. Not only that, but you have blocked the scene naturally. Your character is very much alive in you, and you have discovered some very interesting business. This whole process took less than two hours. So taking this first rehearsal as a guide, you can figure how to use the Tape Technique to your best advantage.

Important: Actors, you will make some very interesting discoveries with the Tape Technique. You are going to want to use these discoveries in performance. Sometimes an actor makes a discovery in rehearsal that illuminates the character for her, but conflicts with the director's concept. The actor can still use the discovery by internalizing it, to disguise it so that, while appearing to accept the direction, she still uses what she found useful. But (and this may be the biggest "but" of your career) the director is still the boss. If he tells you to do it differently, do as asked. None of the work you do using the Tape Technique is wasted.

Regardless of what you do on the outside, nobody knows what you're doing on the inside. When someone complained to General Patton, "Your troops don't know your plan," he said, "It's not important that they know. It's only important that I know."

Warning: Some directors want your ideas, but others don't. You can get your way with some directors, but with others you can't. Learn the difference fast.

DISCOVERING THE SET

For students looking forward to more cooperation between directors and actors when creating a piece, discovering the set together would certainly be a creative plus.

The Tape Technique will be helpful to the actors in knowing where they are. After they've got all their givens, they do the first taping. Then, in a dark place, they lay on their backs, eyes closed, as the scene plays back on the recorder. The actors are to watch it on the movie screen of the mind, being careful to note where the characters go, what's in the space—chairs, windows, color of walls, rugs, pictures—and the physical smells and sounds. Afterward, they draw the scene on paper. It is amazing how similar actors' visions of the place usually are.

They always know where they are—Paris, London, an office, a bar, a kitchen, a living room. They know because they went there, and because of the objects they saw there. I always have students make a diagram—in color if possible—of their scene.

Plays have a fourth wall, the one between you and the audience. Every actor must know everything about that wall and what's beyond it. In film there is a "wild wall," a wall of an apartment or office that is on rollers and is moved so the camera and lights can fit, but for the actor, it is still there. In a film, when you look over your shoulder to the audience, it seems like you're looking at the Grand Canyon or a speeding Corvette, but in fact you're on a sound stage, and all you see is a screen. This will become more important as digital imaging is increasingly used to save money on locations and create effects. The actors in *Jurassic Park*, for example, could not see the dinosaurs.

In TV, there is often something you are supposed to see that isn't actually there. You must create that image, and if you're working with someone else, you have to create the image together. If you're supposed to see somebody offstage, for example, know exactly what he looks like—hair, eyes, height, everything. You and your partner have to be in the exact same place, feel the same temperature, hear the same sounds.

I had two actors doing a restaurant scene that wasn't working. I asked each to write on a piece of paper how much the total meal cost. He wrote $14 and she wrote $107. I asked them how they could be doing a scene together when they weren't even in the same restaurant.

In films and plays you have set designers and real props, but in auditions, most showcases and classes, you don't. Some scripts show a diagram of the set, but you don't have to use it. Remember blacking out the stage directions? You can also black out the diagram. This is your place now. You might be more comfortable with the sink down left instead of down right.

Likewise, you may want to change the place of the action to fit your needs. For instance, two students picked a scene with some great dialogue, but it took place in a small car. The actors couldn't stand up. In the showcase we wanted to see movement, so we put the actors in a living room, and the scene worked much better. Don't just change it for the sake of change, however. Do it the way that makes sense to you.

The original set is not "set in stone." As actors get up and move around, they may discover that their Repels-Impels-Compels carry them to different parts of the stage. They may decide to change this blocking, but at least they have a starting point.

Steve Neal, instructor of theater at Barry University in Miami, quickly saw the possibilities of the Tape Technique, and immediately put them to work. Steve was three hours away from his first rehearsal as director of the university's production of *Steel Magnolias* when I introduced him to the idea. I worked with the cast the first night of rehearsals to help them understand the technique. Although the set was not in place, there were drawings, and the set was roughed out. It was an exciting night, and the openness Steve and the cast brought to this new idea was very gratifying for me. It didn't take the cast long to see the advantages of the Tape Technique, and they approached their work with energy and enthusiasm.

I didn't get back to another rehearsal until a week later. The work was going great, and enthusiasm was high. I noticed the set had been adjusted somewhat, and asked Steve about it. I was thrilled when he said that during rehearsals the Repels-Impels-Compels were moving the actors in directions not accommodated by his original set, so he changed it. He said he knew he could redirect the actors to the original plan, but instead he decided to go with the natural, organic blocking that the actors discovered using the Tape Technique.

Steve and the student actors at Barry University were among the first to use the technique in a full-length production, and I was very happy to see how quickly they learned the mechanical aspects and adapted the spirit of the technique.

Chapter Two

Your Job Between First and Second Rehearsals

There's enough work to fill every second between now and your second rehearsal. How much work you do depends on how much you respect yourself as an actor. This is the time when the actors show their class. Nobody's looking over your shoulder. Nobody's around to make you work hard. It's just you and your script.

My feeling has always been that the obligation of leaders was to make leaders out of followers. If that were happening, we would soon be in an anarchistic utopia. In the real world, however, somebody has to lead. Although you're an actor, and your leader is the director/producer, there is a somewhat artificial distance between the two of you. It's like a coach and team. An actor can never tell another actor to work harder. He can only work three times harder, and if that doesn't do it, work six times harder.

In the 1970s I was doing a show at Judson Poets Theater in Greenwich Village. We finished rehearsal one night with a song I was to sing. I have a good voice, but I got cast for my acting. I am not a singer, and my singing that night was terrible. I was sure everybody was going to go home wondering if I could pull it off. I was so ashamed. I went to legendary composer Al Carmines who put that song on tape for me so I could rehearse that night.

I lived on the lower east side (Third and Bowery) in a somewhat residential area. I stood in the kitchen singing, and every time I finished the song, I drew a mark on the refrigerator door. I sang and sang and it was getting late. The marks on the door were more than 150. When I reached 250 marks, the neighbors started throwing things at my windows. One guy screamed, "You sing that song again, I'm blowin' up your building." So at three in the morning, after three hundred rehearsals, I stopped.

The next day at rehearsal, the director said we'd start with the second act. But I asked if we could start with the song I'd blown the day before. He agreed, and there was an almost audible groan from the cast. I got on stage, Al started to play, and I started to sing. I hit that song with so much authority, the whole place became quiet. That moment set the tone for the show.

I tell that story to make a point: Working your heart out pays off—so go ahead and do it. You love and respect your job, and people do notice.

RESEARCH

Since people have three types of memories, actors have three types of research to do: physical, intellectual and emotional.

Physical memory—Do the characters play football? Walk with a limp? Ride horses? Play piano?

Intellectual memory—Do they read comics or Shakespeare, watch cartoons or Masterpiece Theater?

Emotional memory—Are their parents drunks or Mormons, popular or nerdish, divorced or happily married?

I knew that each type of memory is tightly bound, but I got a serious lesson of how they function independently/dominantly at certain points.

Do you remember when Iraq attacked Kuwait in August 1990? The United States sent half a million soldiers to fight a war. I was getting ready for the war to start. It was the first time a war was going to be live on TV. It almost seemed like I was waiting for a football game to start. President Bush said it would begin at 12:15 on Saturday, so I sat in front of my TV in Orlando, Florida, drinking Wild Turkey. It was a rough few weeks. My 19-year-old daughter and her husband were both members of the U.S. Army and had been in Saudi Arabia for a few months. The last letter I had received from her said he was at the front and she was moved up so close that the bombs kept her awake all night. Hussein talked about chemical weapons and biological warfare. Almost one million soldiers faced each other across a line drawn in the sand, and according to the press, the "mother of all wars" would start in five minutes.

CNN showed shots of missiles and tanks. The drama was intense. I'm a career actor, and it was John Wayne time for me. I was in full battle gear with troops waiting for my signal. I was going to take them over the top. My M16 was mowing them down, and shells were bursting everywhere. "Come on men!" I threw a grenade. But at the height of this fantasy, my eyes exploded with tears and I collapsed onto the floor, my body convulsing in heavy sobs I couldn't control. I managed to get back on the couch, but the tears would not slow.

What happened?

The memories are independent. Any type of memory—physical, intellectual or emotional—can dominate the others at any given moment, depending on the stimulus. This happens to people, and your characters are people.

My intellectual memory, or fantasy, was wonderful. The footage on CNN was fuel. The station cut to a clock showing the time left before the war would start, and the image of my lovely blond-haired, blue-eyed daughter in the middle of all that, did me in. This intellectual memory got stomped by an emotional memory. I felt like I was running full speed one way, and in the tick of a clock, I was full speed in the other direction. I had experienced that kind of shift before, but never so forcefully.

The value to the actor in this story is that I had the emotional memory in place. It was mine, but it could have been my character's. Build all the memories for your character. If it had been a movie, that moment would have gotten me an Oscar.

The real magic in a performance comes when one of your character's memories crashes in on the character's reality. It shows in the eyes, the back and the whole body. This moment of truth can have the same effect on an audience as the story I told had on me. If this moment is going to happen to your character, then you must painstakingly build your character's memories: physical, intellectual, and emotional. Look through a scrapbook, family album or diary for some ideas. These memories function on two levels, past and present.

The physical memory, such as a kiss or a slap, plays an important role. One example came up in a recent Los Angeles workshop, which was a special class for international actors. Two of my Japanese students were doing a scene. They had worked the Tape Technique, but today I wanted to try the scene without the tape. The scene is in English, and since I didn't want them fighting the scene and the language, I told them to run through the scene in Japanese.

I don't speak Japanese, so I didn't know how close they were to the lines, but they seemed to be following the emotional flow of the scene well. Then they would forget a line for a minute, pick it up and go on. Late in the scene they really got stuck. I knew one character needed to make a phone call soon, so I side-coached, "Joey, go pick up the phone and call the cops." The actor was so concentrated, he didn't hear me. I told him again. This time he picked up the phone, and right away he said something to her, and the lines started flowing again. Then they got stuck again. I knew they were near the part where she leaves. I side coached, "Sonja, get your coat, put your bag over your shoulder and leave." She took the direction and, as soon as that bag hit her shoulder, she said her line, and the words flowed to the end of the scene. His phone call, and her leaving, were part of the script, so I wasn't giving them blocking.

Although the actors probably knew already, I explained that Joey's hand remembered the lines. I practically watched the lines go from his hand, up his arm, across his shoulder, and out his mouth. The same was true with Sonja. The second that bag hit her shoulder, the lines jumped into her mouth—one aspect of the physical memory at work. This is one reason I stress using props in the scene as early as possible.

The goal is to build your character's memories into your instrument, just like loading a new program into your computer. In rehearsal you were on your feet and moving with it. When you were taping, you had all the energy and emotion from just doing a run-through.

So this is the first time you've been alone with the script. As you read, all that you got from rehearsal—the immersion into your character and the confrontation with other characters—will wash over you and excite your imagination. Those moments that exploded in you during rehearsal will come back in a different way. If you didn't mark those explosive moments in your script earlier, do it now. I mean big emotional moments. Write the emotion next to the line that generated it.

When doing the Tape Technique, the emotions are leading. If you go through the scene six times, for instance, there may be fifteen emotions written. No matter how many there are, take out your thesaurus and look up the emotions. Those colors/words in the thesaurus help you discover varying degrees of your character's emotion.

Never skip words you don't know. Use a dictionary! When you see all the degrees/colors of intensity involved with that emotion, you may conclude that the emotional explosion actually started to build two lines before you originally thought it did.

You see now how the emotion built up to that powerful moment. You may also see a word in the thesaurus that shows what happened after the explosion—a word that shows how the emotion subsided and changed into the next emotion. Remember your character doesn't physically display the emotion in the same way you do.

Emotions don't just pop out of the blue; they build, explode, subside, and change into the next one. In the story I told about the Persian Gulf War, I said I was going full speed in one direction, and in the tick of a clock I was full speed in the other. If anybody had been watching me, they would have seen my apartment getting sloppier, my eyes turning redder and my body becoming tenser. In my mind I was having a good time, but everything else about me was showing the emotional strain. Anybody watching would have said, this guy is about to crack, he's losing it. The build-up, the progressive intensity of my anxiety would have been obvious to everybody but me. Any idiot can get into an angry moment and scream for two minutes. The good actor will lead us up to it, take us through it and then lead us out of it into the next emotion.

In an Orlando workshop two women were doing a scene about a homeless woman who goes into a fancy New York restaurant. The woman ran through an angry speech about living on the streets. The scene went well, but something was missing. I asked the actress what her primary emotion was, and she said anger. I handed her a thesaurus, told her to look up "angry," and read it out loud.

Here's what she found:

Angry

1. alienated, bigger, emotional, hurt, jealous, offended, provoked, resentful, upset
2. bellicose, belligerent, combative, contentious, hostile, militant, pugnacious, quarrelsome, warlike
3. ferocious, fierce, furious, heated, intense, savage, severe, terrible, vehement, vicious, violent
4. aggravated, annoyed, cross, enraged, excited, fuming, furious, hot, incensed, indignant, irate, mad, provoked, teed off
5. see hot tempered

As soon as she finished reading this list I told them to start the scene. This time, there were many new colors to her emotion. It was obvious to the actors in the scene, and to every workshop member, how much richer the work was using this valuable tool.

OK. So some other colors came in. Remember, all games are won by one point, one run, one goal, one basket. Likewise, parts are won by that one extra color, and since you don't know how many colors the other actors brought to the audition, you better bring every one you possibly can.

Now you need to find out how your character will physically

express certain emotions, and that can only come from research. Remember, the difference between the amateur and professional actor is the amount and type of research. The keys to that treasure vault are given circumstances. The writer gave them to you, so use them.

Recently two actors were nominated for the Academy Award for Best Actor. One was a very popular, hard-working Hollywood actor, and everybody was sure he would win. The other was basically unknown. Both actors, oddly enough, had played handicapped people in wheelchairs. The unknown Irish actor won the award.

This quote from a newspaper might help explain the judges' decision. "To ensure authenticity, Day Lewis spent the entire seven weeks of shooting in a wheelchair. He also mastered the technical difficulties of the role to such an extent that he was actually able to write and paint with his left foot."

I am always awestruck when student actors tell how they do little or no research for a character. They seem to think they'll get by on charm alone.

Research can take many directions. If you're playing a psychiatrist, it may mean studying the latest psychiatric techniques for hours in the library, or hanging out in bars where psychiatrists converge. You might start therapy sessions to gain first-hand knowledge of the profession. One actor playing a psychiatrist had business cards made, and he told new people he met that he was a psychiatrist. One woman asked him what he charged. He told her four hundred dollars an hour. She wanted to hire him.

Good roles will have you playing heroic or tragic people. It is not easy to be a hero or a tragic character. Only extraordinary people reach such highs and lows of the human condition, and the price they pay is great. More than likely you will not pay that price yourself, but with hard work and dedication, you can earn the right to portray such a person. One actress playing a blind woman, for example, wore special contacts that made her functionally blind. She learned to read braille. This in-depth research and her willingness to work hard earned her the right to portray this character. Living in a wheelchair or making yourself functionally blind gives you the feeling that you have earned the right to portray such a person. You will need that determination if you are going to have the confidence necessary to play such a part properly.

GIVEN CIRCUMSTANCES

Before you can do any serious character work, you must know everything you can about the character, as described in the script. It's impossible to do a part correctly without reading the entire script and getting all the "given circumstances," – the facts about your character. These circumstances are in the script directly (Joe is a tall young man with a patch over his left eye, which he lost in a fishing accident when he was three) and indirectly (Sally: "Mary is so afraid of men. Her father was a drunk and raped her for three years before he got caught. She was only eight the first time."). These given circumstances – one physical and direct and the other psychological and indirect – may come before or after your scene.

One illustration of how working without all the given circumstances can change an interpretation came up in a workshop I taught in Portland, Oregon. Two actors played a scene between old friends who hadn't seen each other in a long time. The characters had a few beers and shared some memories about an old friend. One character mentioned a bad smell in the house, and the other one said he burned something while cooking. At one point a hat box was mentioned. The friends arranged to meet again soon, and they parted. I told the actors to read the entire script, noting all the given circumstances. Next week at rehearsal I asked them if reading the whole play changed their interpretation. They both laughed. It seems that what was really happening was, the old buddy in for the visit, and the other guy they talked about, had been given a contract to kill their old friend. Also, they found out that the guy they had come to kill had found out about their plan. And to top it off, the bad smell was the missing pal's head hidden in the hat box.

Having all the given circumstances can greatly change the way you play a scene. It won't always alter your choices as dramatically as in this example. Any diversion, however, means you violated the script, and being true to the text is a professional actor's first obligation. If you're going to be a professional actor, learn how to deal with a script—the whole script. As you read the script, highlight and make a list of the "givens." Once you discover all the circumstances in your script, you can dig in and start some serious character work. Here are a few games to get you started.

Character Game I: Scrapbook

From your list of given circumstances, start to build a photo file of everything given, and then work your imagination.

Suppose a given circumstance is that your character comes from a large family in the Midwest. None of the family members is in the script, but they are still your family, and you are still from a small Midwestern town. So using old books, magazines and photos, find a picture of each person in your family: Mom, Dad, your fifteen-year-old brother, your twelve-year-old brother and your ten-year-old sister. Find a picture of your school, your town, your hangout, your best friend, your dog, your house, your room, and anything else that's significant.

Put this idea into full use. Get pictures of all those memories. Make them concrete, physical. Make a scrapbook for your character. Add pictures, match books, a key from your first car—use your imagination. If you are talking about Mary, your high school girlfriend, have some pictures of Mary. Don't let anything be fuzzy about her, and don't use a picture of your real high school girlfriend. You're from Philly, and a Philly school girl is very different from a Rocky Comfort, Missouri, school girl. You'd be using incompatible images and emotions, and they can't ring as true. Ideally, you could get a yearbook from a small-town high school and pick out a girlfriend. Just studying her picture would probably make my point. You may never have thought about that, but you must see it's true. If not, think about it. If I haven't convinced you yet, I'll keep trying. So much of today's acting is shallow and lazy, not necessarily at the top, across the board.

Character Game II: Dress the Part

If you have any sense of adventure, you occasionally dress out of character. Even if you don't, you have probably noticed that people treat you differently when you're all dressed up than they do when you're in a bathing suit. So if you want to make some discoveries about your character, dress like him, and go to a place he would. As soon as you land a role, figure out how your character would dress. Get an outfit and wear it immediately—even go out in it. If you're doing a period piece, however, think about it. We wouldn't want them throwing a net over you. But, if you're conservative and the character is punked out, go for it. There are not too many conservative actors; they are more likely to go the other way. Always dress like the character at rehearsal.

I know you don't get your wardrobe right away, but scrounge something. The idea of waiting till just before opening or shooting to get your costume is stupid. Take the initiative and find something. It will help. The same goes with props and objects. Get them working for you as soon as you find them. Think a cane might be cool? Try one in a rehearsal. A baseball cap, a yo-yo, whatever, give it a shot. You may later throw the idea out, but try it for now.

Character Game III: Marooned

Suppose you're marooned on a desert island. You can have one of each in the following list. Where it applies, answer these questions. What color is it? How much does it weigh? How does it look, taste, feel, smell, sound, etc. Be specific. Choose one for you and one for your character.

a camera	a house
a motorcycle	a photo
a meat	a toy
a fish	a statue
a drug	a tree
a magazine	a cigarette
an animal	a weapon
a movie	a TV show
a vegetable	a book
an ice cream	a flower
a computer	a pen
a friend	a drink
a car	a beer

Put the lists you made for you and your character side by side and see where they differ. Most parts are type cast, so you're not doing that much when you figure out how you are like your character. Start looking for where you are different from your character. Now you know what you have got to work on.

You can't be out there without a mate. What does he or she look like? How tall? What color eyes? What color hair? Come on, describe this dream! I'm sure you've thought about this person. Now write it out like a letter to Santa Claus, don't leave anything to chance. Describe this person in every detail, and I do mean every detail. Get carried away.

Notice that I didn't include a pet on this list. I'm not a pet person, but if a pet person had made this list, a dog or cat would have been right at the top. So what? Here's so what. Suppose I get a character who is a pet person. He's got a dog he loves, and it's all through the script. I've got work to do. I've got to go to the pound and get a dog, and then learn how to love it.

Character Game IV: One-Word Keys

Korea was just one word in a 120-page movie script, but it led me to a solid week of research that yielded invaluable character information.

I had a starring role in a B movie about a giant lawnmower that ate people on a golf course. Some of you know *Blades*, and you might stop reading right now, but before you do, let me explain a few realities of the business. Now maybe you're independently wealthy, or you got a series your first week in L.A. Maybe you're a saint, who bleeds for his art and would never do a B flick, but some of the actors you admire have done them. You may get two lines in a Spielberg flick, but in a B picture, you can star. I've worked on big and small shows. Big is better, but work is work. As the star of a film, you have the same obligations whether the show cost a million or seventy million dollars. Everybody's counting on you. The quarterback at East Tennessee State University has the same responsibilities as the quarterback at Notre Dame, and they both have a shot at the big time. Starring in any movie is worth a year in class.

My director was a first-time director, just out of film school and primarily an editor. Perhaps he has looked back at that film and thought of many things he would have done differently. It is common for first-time directors to overdirect actors. So, the only scene I'll take credit for is my death scene. Not even a first-time director is going to tell you how to scream when you're getting your legs chewed off by a giant lawnmower. (Gee, sorry I spoiled it for you.)

We had a week to rehearse the film, and my scenes boiled down to a day or two. We actors were forbidden to get together to rehearse on our own. The way I go on about rehearsing, you can guess how I felt about that. We would sneak out and rehearse on our own.

Okay, so back to Korea. I didn't come into the film for the first week of shooting, so I did my homework. I read lawnmower manuals and learned about different types of grass. I read books like *How to Build and Maintain a Golf Course* and *Getting Along with Your New HXP 17,000Z 12 Blade Super Mower*. I also worked on the script and played golf, which I love. I wrote a bio and synopsis about my character's father, and used all the techniques in this book. At night I would be in my room with pictures of mowers, golf courses and grass samples hanging on my wall, analyzing the script. Everyday I played eighteen holes of golf.

One night I went through all my scenes and I came upon one. We were packing my van with guns and grenades, and I saw where my character throws a package to another character, who asks "What's this?" I say, "Plastic explosives left over from the war." She says, "Nam," and I say "No, Korea." This one word "Korea," had not really gotten my attention on prior readings of the script. My character was a soldier. So the next day I went to the Cape May Library, where I found some great research material. I got books on the war and its major battles, and a book by the most decorated soldier to serve in Korea. I patterned a big piece of my character on him. He was amazing, although he started as a private in Korea, he was a general by Vietnam. From the books about the battles with maps and all, I got an overall feel of what that war was like. I learned in one day 30,000 Chinese were killed trying to take one hill. The bodies were piled high, and they still kept coming. The temperature was below zero for weeks and weeks. Food was short. From one book, I got the personal experience of one GI, and it was awesome. So my character was a warrior, a real one. He knew about war, and in this script he is at war with this lawnmower.

After reading all this, I went out the next day to enjoy my golf game. On the first hole I bent over to tee up, and a chill shot up my back that I'll never forget. It was like a razor blade peeling the skin off me. I realized how vulnerable I was to attack in that posture. I started seeing that mower behind every bush. As a warrior, I saw that golf course as I had never seen it before. It was now a battlefield. Everywhere there were attack routes, defensive positions, retreat routes, lines of fire. From that day on, I never felt safe out there. I stopped playing golf and went around the course, moving between trees. Instead of walking the fairways with a five iron on my shoulder and a song in my heart, I was ducking, running and crawling on my belly.

That one word, in a scene much more low key than many others, was the key to my character. So, you never know. The actor sees all the meaty stuff, and it needs work. But sift through that script: every word could be the missing key. It is a rule of good writing that every line advances the plot. Look at each one. The tendency is to get caught up in the big stuff—the meaty and the dramatic—and miss some really interesting moments. You will serve yourself and your career well to not believe there is such a thing as a "throw-away line." Make the most of every line.

I ran into one of my Orlando students one day. We went for coffee. She had a reading in four hours at Universal Studios. I said, "Let's blow you out of here. Go get the lines and work on them." She said, "It's only two lines, no problem."

That is the dumbest thing I hear from actors. Question: How do you get four lines? Answer: By working as hard on two lines as you would on twenty lines or two hundred lines.

Character Game V: Spy

Here's a game I give my students. If you're walking down the street, and you see someone who makes you think of your character, spy on that person. Follow him into a restaurant, and get the table next to his. How does this person sit? Does he look around, smoke, read a newspaper? How does he speak to the waitress? Which hand does he hold his fork in? Try to start a conversation with this person. If he works in a store, pretend you want to buy something. Talk to him and observe. I tell students that everybody they meet is research material. Spy on them.

There is another way to spy on your character, only this time you do it from the inside.

First-Person Synopsis

Continuity is vital to the flow of an actor's performance. To give your performance continuity, you must know the history of your character's life. The easiest way is to write a first-person synopsis of your character's life, from before he or she enters the story and beyond. Suppose your character, Bobbie, enters the story when he runs into an old girlfriend at a bar in Fort Lauderdale. Your synopsis might go something like this.

> *I recognized her right away. She was always hot. She was hot when I was doing her when we were fourteen, and she's even hotter now. Red dress, white wine, tall, tan and blond. I walk up and say hello, she smiles, we start talking. We move to a booth, a couple of drinks later we're in her Jaguar, doing lines of coke in the parking lot. She gets a few bumps and starts telling me about how she got mixed up with the mob. She's got fourteen keys in the trunk and let's go to New York. I said cool, but I got to make a phone call. I'm in the bar about five minutes, and when I come out two apes are shoving her into the trunk of the Jag and they roar off.*
>
> *CUT TO: Int. Jaguar, night*

So you're out of the script for the next five pages. When you come back, you are cruising down the street when you see the red Jaguar parked outside a house. But where were you for those five pages? Please don't tell me you were in your trailer. Many times the script won't tell you, but if you want continuity in your performance you will want to know. That's why you're writing this synopsis. So to continue.

I didn't know what to do. I did jot down her license number, then I wandered back into the bar to get a drink. I was buzzing on the blow, and a whole bunch of stuff had just been dumped on me. Not the least of which being that I might get killed. Four frozen double Stolis later, I called a friend of mine. He was a dealer who might know her, and knew what I might be getting myself into. He met me at the bar and after a few drinks, and a few toots in the john, I saw how it was probably going to play. We agreed to meet in the morning. Johnny knew "the boys," and figured if she wasn't dead, there might be a scam we could run that would net the babe, the blow, and a nice tour of the continent. I went back to the hotel, but couldn't sleep, so I sat on the beach and thought about whether I was really bored enough with life to try to take fourteen keys and a hot blond from the Mafia. By the time the sun started burning my eyes, I was sure I was. So I went to meet Johnny. We got together early. The first part of the plan was to cruise the neighborhood around the mob's house, and see if there was any sign of the Jag. Then find out if the blow was still in the trunk. So I cruised down the boulevard and there was the Jag. I checked the license to make sure it was the right one.

So now you know where you were for the last five pages and you flow right into the scene. You have to be consistent with the script, but anytime you're out of it, have some fun. Just know where you were every moment and what you were feeling. I like to write some of the dialogue in these off-script adventures too, like the scene with Johnny in the bar.

BEGINNING-MIDDLE-END

The time between rehearsals is a great time for actors. You're on your own, and the things you learn can set your imagination on fire. You can't wait until your next rehearsal to find out how the script is going to come out, when you're working the Tape Technique with your partner.

But since this is an accelerated schedule—I mean we are doing work that would normally be spread out over a longer period—let's pack it with some more techniques, exercises and ideas.

One of the things we want to discover is the beginning, middle and end of the piece. When you get a scene or script, it can seem complicated, and you will want to simplify it. Here's a way.

Every scene must have a beginning, a middle and an end. For example, you go to your lover's house (beginning), something happens and you fight (middle), and you make up (end).

It's not always that simple, but you get the idea. The Tape Technique will be a big help with this. The first time you practice the Tape Technique and each time thereafter, you will notice because of what you say or hear, your emotion will change—sometimes radically. Those moments are keys; they will probably mark the Beginning-Middle-End for you.

The goal here is to break the scene up, to make it easier to work with. It's like slicing a pizza. Picking up a large pizza and eating it whole would be very tricky.

All artists do this in one way or another. Musicians will approach a symphony by first playing the whole piece to get a feel for it. Then they break it down into movements, stanzas, sections, beats. Dancers break a piece down into sections, segments, phrases, etc.

In its simplest form, a play begins with Act I. Act II is the middle, and Act III, the end. But movies aren't that clean sometimes, and TV can be less so. I will concentrate on the scene, which is the basis of most actors' training. Since the scene is plucked from a total work and is only a few minutes (usually three minutes for auditions) of the entire play, it poses problems not explored so intently by an actor doing the whole play. Difficulties within the scene are solved by the work done in other parts of the play. The work done in Act I may provide the answer to this scene in Act II, but the student working on an Act II scene won't be doing all that work on Act I, so it's intense.

The actor has to solve the problems of the whole play in this one scene. Finding the beginning, middle and end is the first step. Hopefully, if you picked a scene properly, the beginning is the beginning, and the end is the end. That is, the beginning has a logical start, and the end resolves whatever conflict came in the middle, but

Where's the middle?
Where does the middle begin?
Where does it end?

When you have that, you have broken the scene down to a much more workable format. To find those moments, look for the emotional explosions (the overpowering Repels-Impels-Compels) while doing the Tape Technique.

It would help to use the Tape Technique on a scene or two with the same characters from another part of the play. Before and after, if they exist. Just tape the scene, get up and let the emotions fly. Any decent actor would take a hard look at those scenes anyhow. This way you get to feel them. Even if you only use the Tape Technique on them once, you're ahead.

PHYSICAL PREPARATION

It's getting close to second rehearsal and you've done a lot of work. You did emotional homework and your character research homework, using given circumstances, and your creative imagination. You used the ideas in the character games. You found the beginning, middle and end of the scene, and cut it as close to three minutes as possible. You have also found a few other props and costume pieces you want to try. So what's left?

Prepare yourself physically. For example, if your scene has some slaps, punches, knockdowns, or falls of any kind, there are a few things you must think about.

Sometimes in a script you get slapped, punched, pushed, or otherwise physically manipulated. In an audition, if you're reading with a casting director, a stage manager or another actor, he or she may not fake the slap or hit. You have to create your reaction with all the force of a real hit. If it knocks you down, go down. If you don't know how to fall, learn. There is a technique for getting knocked down. Don't wait till you have to, and then just "go for it." You can bust your butt. Find somebody who knows the technique and learn it. No matter how good you get, you may still get a small bruise. It goes with the territory.

Negative Empathy

I once did a play where I was a bad guy. At one point I was supposed to get slapped in the face by an actress. I (my character) was really a villain, and the audience hated me. It was a thrust stage, and the audience was close enough to lick me on three sides. Sometimes I heard them say things like, "They ought to kill that S.O.B." So they wanted to see me get slapped. The problem was that the actress would sometimes get carried away with her part. She would slap me so hard that there was a big hand print on my face. I told her one night, "If you break my jaw, there's no second act."

All actors have to be ready to take a slap or get pushed around a little. We're not made of glass, and certain parts call for some spills. The problem comes when the audience, instead of saying "Good, she slapped that bastard," says, "My god, that poor actor. Look, his face is swelling up."

At that point it has turned to negative empathy, and the play is hurt. It's good that her emotions, her creative side was working so strongly, but when you forget that it's a play, you lose the audience, and keeping them is the reason you're there.

Early in my career I did *Cat on a Hot Tin Roof*, and at one point I took a swing at Maggie with my crutch. I got so worked up I caught her in the side of the head. She was good. She finished the scene from the floor, but it was definitely negative empathy.

Two-Eyed Theory

One eye is creative and emotionally sensitive (the left one, if you're interested), and the other is practical and logical (the right). I read somewhere that in the early 1900s when troupes of actors would go from town to town, the actors could do King Lear's "Blow, winds, blow" and count the members of the audience at the same time. They had to, because they were splitting the house, and the promoters would cheat them if they didn't.

Left brain, right brain is a fact. The left eye is controlled by the right brain. It is the part of the brain that deals with the creative/emotional side of our nature. The right eye is controlled by the left side of the brain, which deals with logic, numbers and the more practical side of our natures. Most people are left- or right-brain dominant. There is a book called *Whole Brain Thinking*, and an actor must be able to access both sides of his brain while acting. He can't get excited and stab somebody. It's only a play. In the sword fight in *Hamlet*, an actor I was working with got his ear cut. Blood was flowing down the side of his head. When he came offstage, he was angry because it was his upstage ear. It seemed funny to me at the time, but the blood was real. If he had left his ear out there, it wouldn't have been funny at all.

This is a grand and irreconcilable paradox of acting. You forget who you are and become the character. At the same time, remember who you are, and be professional and technically correct. It seems impossible, but good actors do it every day.

Suppose you're doing a scene where your mother is dying. She means everything to you. You hold her and cry. Then something clicks: You realize you've had your back to the audience for too long. You gently shift dear old Mom's head around so your face is out to the audience. The tears never stop, and the pain is constant.

Sensory Preparation

Physical preparation also means sensory preparation. For example, I don't have to tell you how powerful smell is when it comes to stimulating people. Okay, so you weren't hungry—not a thought of food in your mind. You walk past this pizza joint, and suddenly you need a slice real bad. Right? Another time, you're just hanging out, feeling good, and some guy walks by wearing your ex-boyfriend's cologne. Now you're totally depressed or reaching for the phone. Right?

I was doing *Watch on the Rhine*, by Lillian Hellman at The New Rose Theater in Portland, Oregon. I was saying good-bye to my wife, who just had a long speech to some other people in the room about why she was leaving me. As she's walking out she turns and says, "Good-bye, Teck." I have been sitting in an armchair down left. I am dressed in this great tuxedo—double breasted with satin lapels. I look up and say, "Good-bye." A tear falls from my left eye and runs down the left satin lapel. A short pause, and I say, "Martha." Now a tear falls from my right eye and runs down that satin lapel. I'm doing this five nights a week, and twice on Sundays.

I was able to do this with such precision because I first used smell. Estée Lauder was the favorite perfume of someone very close to me. I was using her to recall an affective memory. This is tragically funny, but instructional, so I'll explain.

The first time I decided to use the perfume in the play, I almost forgot to put it on. Less than a minute before my entrance, I remembered the perfume. I whispered some "excuse me's" to my cast members and tiptoed behind the set to the dressing room to grab the bottle of Estée Lauder. I slapped it on like after-shave. When I rejoined my cast members waiting backstage, the whispered remarks were priceless. Estée is a heavy perfume. Before we even entered, the small theater filled up with the smell of the perfume. When the lights came on, I could see people turning in their seats, trying to figure out who was stinking up the place. After that I put small amounts up my nose, and that worked much better.

The perfume helped the affective memory, but to get the tears precisely at the second I said "Good-bye" and "Martha," I used something mechanical. I had noticed at the first rehearsal in the theater, after the lights were set, that a Fresnel light above my chair was being reflected in my wedding ring. That's when I came up with the business of inspecting the ring as she talked of leaving me. It looked like I was sadly ruminating on a failed marriage. Indeed I was, but on the other hand, I was turning the ring a certain way so I could take the dull reflection of the spotlight and make it highly spectral to the point that it irritated my eye to tear. So the perfume helped the affective memory, and by aiming the ring at one eye, and then the other, I could control the flow and timing of each teardrop.

If there is a moral to this, I suppose it's that there are many ways to get a good performance, and if you are focused on that goal, ideas will come to you.

Music

Music is and always has been a big part of life, but portable CDs make today different. Louis XIV had a chamber orchestra follow him around the garden at Versailles. Today, any person working in a car wash has good music.

When you look at your script, who are you listening to at that moment? I couldn't imagine doing homework without some kind of music. Right there in the script, as your character plots that murder, suicide, that fight against the bad guys, what's on your Walkman or home sound system? Clock your day. How much of it has music going on? It's playing in the store, your house, coming out of somebody's room, and the car. When you rehearse, have music. Maybe you're at your friend's in the scene, and he's playing a rap CD that you hate. You see what I'm saying? Music is always there. Get it into your acting.

This is one major reason I don't let my students do scenes that are more than five years old. Listen to some '40s music and then some Thrash Metal or hard core, Ministry maybe. Don't come to me with '40s and '50s stuff. Let the dead be grateful. Ninety percent of scripts being done are being written by people who are alive. There is a Beastie Boy in Neil Simon somewhere. The tempo of the scripts is today's. Listen to the beat; it changes. Even if somebody today writes a period piece, her blood is flowing to today's tune. Think of the clothes they wore in those days. Think of how we dress today. You would have been arrested if you wore then what we wear now.

A side note: There was a time when you got arrested and went to jail for acting. People still acted though. It's obviously a need, *a need to be good*. Use everything. Tunes are part of life. They are part of acting. If your character is into opera, don't pretend to love it. Love it. You don't have to marry it, but love it while you must.

Chapter Three

Directors and the Whelan Tape Technique

Unless you are just beginning your career, the Whelan Tape Technique is going to be very alien. Your teachers and past experience, for the most part, have you conditioned to look at the actor-director relationship in a certain way. A way which, like the covered wagon and the lawnmower you pushed, served their purposes well at that time in history. Technology came along and replaced them, advanced them. What I'm offering you is a way to use technology and get better performances from actors, while challenging your creativity to the maximum.

I was doing a show called *Wanted* at Judson Poets Theater in New York. Larry Cornfeld was my director, and Al Carmines wrote, played and conducted the music. Between them they have a wall filled with Tonys. I played Jesse James, a kind of composite father of the revolution. It was a very meaty role. All the opportunity in the world for an actor to chew up the scenery (overact).

I was ranting and raving from day one. Larry left me alone. After about three days of this, I walked up to him and said, "Larry, I'm getting a little self-conscious about all this yelling." There came a sparkle into his eyes as he twirled one point on his finely waxed mustache. With a soft smile, he said, "That's nice" and walked away.

I'm sure Larry has no idea how much that directorial patience has affected my acting and directing career. He trusted me. He could have told me that the first or surely the second day. He could have walked up to me and said, "All that yelling is too much. It won't work." He would have been right, and I would have hated him, thinking all through the rehearsals and the run that this stupid director had robbed me of my brilliant conception of character. As it was, he gave me a chance to find it, and I did. Give your actors that trust. In the Whelan Tape Technique the director takes a minimal role early in the work. I can tell you from my own experience that that trust can have a profound and lasting effect on a young artist.

FIRST REHEARSAL WITH THE TAPE TECHNIQUE

First, familiarize yourself with the techniques outlined on pages 5-21. Now, to explain how you can use the technique as a director, I will go through a step-by-step rehearsal, using two actors in a three-minute scene. With that understanding, you can then apply the Tape Technique to the whole cast, doing plays, movie scripts, TV shows. The first rehearsal must be long enough to allow at least four complete tapings and run-throughs. This whole process should take about two hours.

Before the First Taping

The actors walk in the door. They have a script they have read, which contains a three-minute scene they want to do but have not worked on. They made a list of all given circumstances related to their character, and then blacked out all stage directions the first time they saw them.

A Few Basic Rules for the Director

As director, the hardest thing you will have to do is do nothing at first. Your talent and creativity will be truly challenged later, but in the beginning, you are only there to observe and occasionally side-coach. Remember this work is new, if you give it a chance you will be well rewarded. Don't give the actors any blocking, business or line readings. Don't even tell them where you think the piece should go. Think of them as new and clever pets. Just put them down on the floor, and be amused by what they do.

However:

1. Forbid them to memorize lines.
2. Make sure they are aware of all major given circumstances.
3. Make sure they only do one take when taping. (Don't forget the sound check.)
4. Black out any stage directions.
5. Go over the Repels-Impels-Compels with them—*the idea, not specific moments.*
6. Make sure they never try to memorize lines. This is important enough to be repeated. The whole idea is that everything grows at once. If they sit down and memorize the lines with only their minds, they will blow many of the possible gains from this technique.
7. Don't ever let them use the same taping twice.

Have them tape the scene. Then have them get up and act it out following the guidelines set up at the beginning of this book.

By the way, don't expect too much on the first run-through. This is new for them too. Experienced actors may tend to jump around as they get used to the freedom. It will take them a few times through to lose the performance imperative. New actors will be stiff at first, and it will take them a few times through before they start to move naturally. This situation only comes up the first time they meet the technique.

Between the First Run-Through and Second Taping

Because of all the new-found freedom and unfamiliarity with the technique, the actors may have been "third eyeing" themselves during the first run-through. In these cases, they tend to focus on what they did wrong, the negative. You must turn that around. One moment of real connection to the characters' emotions is what should be talked about and thought about. These moments have a natural tendency to want to expand. If the actors don't remember those moments, you will. A question about that moment should jog their memory. If not, let it go, and just run it again. Never let them talk about when they didn't connect. Negativity is a waste of time.

When the scene has ended, you might ask them how it felt. You'll get answers ranging from "weird" to "interesting." Some may say, "I didn't like it. I want to use the script." Remember that the script is a shield between the actors, not much emotion gets in or out. Using the Tape Technique, the emotions are in immediate and direct contact. There is no ducking behind the script if things get too intense.

You can ask if there was a moment when they felt really connected to their character. More than likely you saw it happen. If they say no, just let it go. If they say yes, ask them when. Don't let them talk too much, but a little is okay. Keep your comments to only a very few questions.

You probably noticed a moment when the actor had a strong Repel, Impel or Compel. You saw them want to get up, sit down, walk away, or go to the other actor. The rule about stage directions being blacked out is so important to this. Most actors' training breeds insecurity. Actors sometimes jump at anything that gives them a hook on the character, even something as stupid as a stage direction left over from some other actor and some other director at some time in the past. I've been acting forever but I still know the panic of creation.

The point is, I watched an actress try to get off a chair six times. Everything in her was standing up except her mind and consequently her body. It was so obvious that she wanted to stand it was almost comical. Everybody in the class saw it happening. When I asked her why she didn't take that Impel, she said the stage directions had her get up at a later line. She had somehow missed my speech about blacking those stupid things out and doing it any way she wanted. This was the first time she had worked the Tape Technique.

When you are dealing with actors negating genuine impulse for any other reason, it is best left alone at this point. Do not address the particular moment. It will sound like direction, and the actor might lock into it, missing a chance at a much more interesting choice. A general statement such as "I thought I noticed moments when you wanted to move, but you didn't take it. Am I right?" If they say no, again let it go. If they say yes, ask "Do you remember where?" After they tell you, ask why they didn't take it. The answer is usually, "I thought," and then something about the past or future of the script. This means they were in their heads, as actors, making judgments. This critical left brain interference with the creative process has to be discouraged. Simply remind them that the object of the exercise is to get in touch with their characters' feelings and to go with any impulse they get. That is more than enough talk at this stage. Quite often, I'll just tell them to tape it again as soon as they finish the first run-through. No talk at all.

DURING THE SECOND RUN-THROUGH

Because of the contact in the first run-through, the actors will start to open up more this time, emotionally and physically. Leave them alone as much as possible. Side coach only when you see them negating strong Repels-Impels-Compels. Tell them to go with the emotion, follow their impulses.

Note: Basic side-coaching: Keep your voice low, and tell them, "Never look out. Don't break your concentration, make the adjustment, and go on."

Sometimes an actor, because of insecurity, will overwork a single prop. Don't bust them right away. Give them a chance to correct it. If it goes on forever, just side coach: "Don't make a career out of the blanket."

That's about it, except an occasional "How do you feel saying that?" "How do you feel when he or she says that to you?" Again, stay way back. Do not give any business, blocking or line readings.

Between the Second and Third Tapings

At this point, you should basically do the same as you did between the first and second taping, or say nothing. If you saw a nice, rich response to a Repels-Impels-Compels, mention it. We all need encouragement, but be sure to tell the actor that it might change, and let it!

THIRD RUN-THROUGH

This third run-through is discussed in chapter one (page 11). Just keep this run-through short and sweet.

Between the Third and Fourth Run-Throughs

Ask if they learned anything about their characters or relationships. If they say no, let it go. If they say yes, ask them what. These shared insights can help.

FOURTH RUN-THROUGH

This time you will use the Pause Technique. This is a very powerful tool and you are fully in control. Almost every problem you've seen the actors having up to this time will be solved here, and you never have to open your mouth, just press the button. Some lazy first choices will be abandoned, and new and exciting choices will be found. The moments that had been working really well will get much richer. This is the time we have been working toward. The first steps were vital explorations, but the Pause Technique is where major breakthroughs occur. Take all the time you want, but be sure that their concentration doesn't slip. If it does, guide them back with side-coaching.

Because this is such an important technique, I put it in the front of the book in the actors' section. Please refer to it there on page 14. Then come back and give the Pause Touch a chance, it too solves some major problems.

WHELAN TAPE TECHNIQUE WITH PAUSE TOUCH

I picked one half of this up in Jo Forsberg's workshop at Second City, Chicago. It's a touch technique used there in improvs. I always use it in my scene study classes. It is great. Usually you have to wait until the actors have their lines down cold before you can use it, but by bringing in the Tape Technique, it can be used in the first half hour of work.

After, say, three times through with Tape Technique, you and the actors have loosened up some and are relating to each other and the material. In the Pause Technique you are waiting for an emotional build, but in this case the actors have to make physical contact before a speech.

Note: The tendency here is to play tag and cling close together. If that happens, tell them "no hands." If they go to all feet, say "no feet." Encourage them to keep the Repels, Impels and Compels. That will have them moving around some.

As the director, before you start the tape for the first line or speech, make sure they make physical contact. It is not necessary for them to contact on every line, just before every speech. Actor A makes contact with actor B. Maybe A puts her head on B's shoulder. Then A's speech plays on the tape. A takes the appropriate Repels-Impels-Compels. If A is repelled, then B must catch up with her and make contact. Maybe a gentle stepping on the toe at that point. B's speech is played. Go through the whole scene like this.

This can turn a very serious scene into comedy. As the actors get more inventive, knees, butts, elbows, everything comes into play. Comedy scenes become hilarious. Don't just let them stand in one place and make dull, routine contact. Let them enjoy it, but do a little side-coaching: "Take that Repel."

After they have the lines, run this contact exercise again without the tape. Have them monitor themselves at that point, but stay on top of them. The energy gets quite high. They get excited and blurt out lines before making contact. Bust them quick! Make them go back and do it right.

Between the Fourth and Fifth Tapings

You will probably want to talk about some of the things you saw going on. The Pause Technique brings out so much emotion. It also has the actors, as they work to stay in character, creating tons of business, much of which will be useful to the production. Take notes, but don't say anything that sounds like a "direction." They will probably come up with something even better.

Caution: The actors are going to want to talk after this. Control this urge. Some short conversation is okay but realize they have just gotten some deep insights into character and relationship.

Don't let it get lost in talk. It's still so fresh. Do everyone a favor and as soon as they finish, set them up to tape immediately. Tell them not to try to remember anything they said or did. That's not the same as telling them not to do it. That's another exercise and comes later.

Before the Fifth Run-Through

The actors are very familiar with the characters, relationships and lines by now. They must guard their concentration if they are to stay in the moment and give their creativity a chance to come up with anything new.

SIXTH RUN-THROUGH

This is not an improv. Do the script!

Just tell the actors to do the scene, no scripts, no tape. Just do what they remember. They may laugh at first, but when they realize you're serious, they may panic. Calm everybody down. It's just an experiment. Fact is, if the props have been there, and their concentration has been good, they know 60 to 90 percent of the dialogue. Put somebody on book, but make sure they know not to give a line until it's asked for.

Some actors get very insecure at this request. They start calling for "line" right away and often. This is just nerves. If they start that "line, line" stuff, just tell them to relax and get into the emotion and work. This is not a test. It's not a performance. It's a first rehearsal. Let them catch their breath. Tell them to take a moment, get into their first emotion, then start again when they are ready.

Two things to remember:

1. They have less and less trouble as they get deeper into the scene.
2. The problems usually come at transition points in the script. Places where their need changes. Once inside a section like this, it will flow again.

When they have finished the scene, you will all be surprised at how much was remembered and how well it flowed. Now you can talk. Just remember what you saw was the result of only two hours of work. Your rehearsal schedule from here is up to you. The work done in this rehearsal has taken the scene way forward.

To the director: If you are working with experienced actors, they understand what they have to do between now and next rehearsal. If you are working with new actors or students, you should explain to them the idea of actors' homework.

To the actor: Actors sometimes go to directors with a question, only to have the director look at them and say, "That's actors' work" and walk away. Beginning actors can feel lost at that answer. It's true directors will sometimes say that because they don't have an answer for your question at that time, but usually it is because it *is* actors' work.

Actors have a lot of homework to do. First and foremost is research. I don't mind repeating: The difference between the amateur and professional actor is the amount and type of research. After they have done some serious research, they have their bios and synopses to write (see below). There are memories to build, prior or future relationships with the other characters to investigate. Improvs are not only okay, but great for this. Many exercises and variations on the Tape Technique can be worked.

Remind them their homework includes analyzing the script. "Analyze" does not mean memorize lines—that is still forbidden. Part of analysis is going over the script, and in those places where they got a major Repels-Impels-Compels, noting that emotion next to the line. Then they should look it up in the thesaurus, becoming aware of all the different shapes/shades of that emotion. Remember, actors, if you don't know the meaning of some of those words, look them up.

So if they did their homework, one more intense rehearsal should have this scene up on its feet and running. After that, it's just going deeper into the emotions and refining the physical expression of those emotions. This will be helped enormously by further research.

How much you use the Tape Technique is up to you, but it should be used until the actors know the lines. Learning the lines is not the *goal*—it is the result of the character awareness that comes from using the technique.

That will happen so quickly that you will be shocked and delighted. Under those circumstances, these actors have a real good handle on the relationship and the dialogue. They found a basic, and for the most part, workable blocking, plus many interesting pieces of business.

Using the Tape Technique with a full production is no problem. I created this technique to use with a cast of seventeen, in a three-act play. The main thing is to have the whole cast present at the first rehearsal. Give yourself enough time to have two full tapings and run-throughs. All the rules for two characters apply to seventeen characters. Even if they only have small parts, they are to stay and watch both tapings and run-throughs. Soon you'll be breaking rehearsals into acts or scenes, but now, for bonding purposes, everybody stays and focuses on the work. After you have broken rehearsals down to scenes, there is no reason why actors involved in a different scene can't do the Tape Technique in another room. I break up the scenes and put the different scenes anyplace I can. Each actor should be running the Tape Technique. I work with one scene for a while then leave the actors on their own while I work with a different scene. I just keep going from scene to scene with an observation here, a suggestion there.

I was doing a sixteen-page voice-over for a tape to accompany a tram tour through some condos in Palm Springs. It was a nightmare. The director was the creative director from the ad agency. He stopped me on almost every word. We were on take 17 of a line on page 2, an hour and a half into the session. When the adman got a phone call and left to take the call, I told the engineer to roll tape. I read all sixteen pages in one shot. We were just starting the playback when the director returned. He didn't say anything, just sat and listened. When it was over, he said, "That's great. We can use 98 percent of that. I guess I should have left you alone. We would have been out of here an hour ago." So leave them alone. They're not going to start talking about basketball just because you leave the room. They're actors.

As a director, when you get a script, you're bound to get ideas about how this should be said and how that should be done. Don't fall in love with it.

Peter Brook tells a story about his first directing job when he made a model of the set and little cutouts of the actors. He sat up all night, moving them here and there, taking hundreds of notes. When he walked into his first rehearsal the next day and started working with the actors, he soon chucked his notes and cutouts in the dust bin, because he realized he was working with actors, not cutouts.

So as you approach your script, do it with an open mind, and come to your first rehearsal with your mind still open. You will be surprised and delighted at how the actors perceive the piece and the characters. In many places, your ideas and theirs will match perfectly. In others, their imagination may leap in exciting and unique ways beyond how you envisioned it. They are, after all, focused on one part only, while you are trying to see the whole. A script is a map. Give the same map to three professional drivers, and they will take different routes but wind up in the same place. In the end, you are the power, and the actors will do it your way. So let them run.

DIRECTORS – SECOND REHEARSAL

Actors show up fresh and ready to work, bursting with ideas generated by the homework they did since the first rehearsal. After actors have done a proper physical and vocal warm-up, the work can begin by taping the scene and then doing a Mirror I, II or III Exercise: This should generate a lot of energy and add to character insight. Follow the exercise with a taping and run-through. If actors have done their homework, they will reach a new dimension and a much greater depth of character penetration. This should excite the actors and you. They should feel rewarded for the hard work and research they did. From here, there are many ways to go. The actors or director can choose whichever most excites their imagination.

"The Phrase That Pays" is a great exercise to work on next. It came out of one of my Orlando workshops, and I've used it with every directing and teaching job I've done since.

The-Phrase-That-Pays Exercise

Two students were working on a scene. In this scene he was doing a sailor, and she owned the waterfront bar. They were hanging out together but having problems. The actors had been at the scene long enough that it should have been flowing better. I was looking for a way to fix it, when I noticed they had a line in common. It was, "I'm not leaving." She says it early in the scene, and he says it later. When I looked at that, I realized that the whole scene was about leaving. So I put them about six feet apart and had them repeat back and forth, "I'm not leaving." I let them go on like that for five or six minutes. It really ripped in places. As soon as I stopped them, I said, "Start the scene." The scene was great. Afterward, I asked them what the exercise did for them. "It grounded the scene for me," they said. These exact words came up when I used this exercise in other cities with other scenes. This is an important exercise. The phrase that pays, find it and use it. It's in that scene somewhere. Sometimes you can lift it straight from the script, but other times you have to bend a word or two.

The scenario I've described is based on a very condensed and intense rehearsal schedule with two dedicated actors and an open-minded director. If all those elements were present, and all my suggestions were followed, the scene would almost be ready to present.

To recap: The actors did

1. Five tapings and five run-throughs to tape.
2. A run-through with someone on book.
3. A lot of hard work between the first rehearsal and this one.

They did lots of research and emotional homework, and they made a scrapbook of their characters' past. They got together and did three or four tapings and run-throughs. They improvised past and future relationships and analyzed the script. If half of that is true, this scene is in great shape by now. From the tapings they already did, and without even trying, they know the lines. That's what they say. To prove that without a doubt, here's how:

Speed-Through

Once you have your lines in pretty good shape, you can find out if you really do know them. Stand with your partner, and say them as fast as you can. Don't take a breath. Don't pause. Don't act. Just say them flat and fast. Any place you stumble is where you are weak. When you really know them you will not stumble anywhere.

A warm-up for this is a speed read-through. Now I don't care how well you think you know the script. When you do a speed read-through, keep your eyes glued to the script. Notice every period, every comma. Stay on the script.

Unless you can do a speed-through, you are in danger of blowing the lines in performance. This is an ultimate test of knowing the lines. Your lines overlap your partner's by a split second. THEREISNOTIMETOBREATHEORTODOANYACTINGTHE WORDSMUSTCOMEOUTOFYOURMOUTHASFASTASYOU CANPOSSIBLYSAYTHEMANDTHENGOFASTERAND FASTER.

You can face each other if you want. Usually I have the actors face front.

Okay. The actors passed the speed-through. Let them run it once just to settle down, and then we will throw them a few more creative curve balls.

Can't Do What You Did

At a certain point in rehearsal the work settles in pretty nicely. The actors have good solid characterizations. The relationships are well developed, and the emotional flow is powerful and correct. It's time to get crazy and have some fun. Tell the cast that for this run-through they cannot do anything they have been doing. They must have a different:

1. Voice and accent
2. Movement, walk and posture
3. Attitude and emotional reaction

I don't remember when I started this exercise, but I do know I've always gotten great results. If it ain't broke, why fix it? Is that what you're asking? The first time I did this exercise, I was probably bored. However, doing the scene immediately after doing this exercise, I saw that besides blowing a ton of fresh air through all of us, it inspired some powerfully unique adjustments and choices in characterization and line readings. Because the dynamic of the piece had been so well established, the actors integrated all these new choices smoothly and naturally.

By this time the director has been totally integrated into the cast. The director's job here is to be a good referee and to make sure the rules aren't broken. This is not easy! If you're a sports fan, you know that when referees know that they have a rough game to call, they call every little infraction at the beginning. This lets the players know they are not going to get away with anything, so they settle down and play by the rules. You must set this same tone early in the exercise.

Actually, using the new accents will do most of the work for you. Since accents are loaded with cultural stereotypes, physical, emotional and intellectual traits come forward quickly. However, the actors have worked for some time, discovering, rejecting and refining their characters. They will have a strong tendency to hang onto or slip back into what they have been doing. Stay on top of them. Every time they repeat business from before or give the same read to a line, stop them. If you bust them every time in the beginning, they will get the message and get into it. After that they will work so hard and have so much fun, the scene should flow. Don't go to sleep. At very emotional moments, they may backslide. As soon as this run-through is completed, just say, "Okay. Do the scene immediately, and whatever happens, happens." It will be fresher, and far better in places than it was before this exercise.

The Laugh Technique

My classes always showcase. I believe all acting classes should have a performance dimension. It is something to work for, a chance to show what you learned. Working with me, there is a point when you are near the end of rehearsals. I use this Laugh Technique after the actors know the lines and usually very near the last rehearsal.

I have the cast do the piece first in class or rehearsal so I can see what they accomplished in their private rehearsals and so the actors and the other students can see the benefits of the technique. Then, I tell the actors to do the piece again, only everything they say is the funniest thing they ever heard. They should laugh as hard as they can all the way through the line and before and after the line. I don't care what the line is about—murder, child abuse, rape. It doesn't matter, it's funny.

The same goes for the other actors: Everything they hear is the funniest thing they ever heard. Stay after them, don't let them slack off. I've gone up and tickled the actors to keep them roaring. It's exhausting, and they will be drained when it's over. The next time they play the scene, it will have many new colors and an appropriate looseness and naturalness.

Some people find it easy to laugh, some find it very hard. But laughter is infectious. When this exercise is working, the whole room is rocking, and that helps the stiff ones. It's up to the teacher to stay on top of the actors. Don't let them continue if they are not laughing loudly at every line. It's work to keep them laughing hysterically at every line, but the results are worth it.

Creative Rehearsal

Three students in Orlando were working on a piece called *Eating Out*, by Marcia Duxcy. It's about three young women. One is anorexic. One is bulimic. And the other does it all, diet pills, bulimia and anorexia.

As written, it is staged with the three girls on a bare stage sitting and talking to the audience. We tried it that way, but it was mostly long monologues that pick up on each other near the end. I wasn't happy with it that static.

For the next rehearsal, I brought the whole class around, and worked the scene as a group therapy session for people with eating disorders. The other members of the class took characters, asking questions, and making statements. We tried that a few times.

At the next rehearsal, I had the actors do the scene as models getting ready for a fashion show—putting on makeup, going behind a screen and changing clothes, continuing their monologues, and coming back on. We ran that a few times. During the next rehearsal I put them in a restaurant. They sat at the table picking at lettuce and sipping Perrier. Then I added a waiter, and four other actors from the workshop became gluttons sitting at a table, ordering and eating every delicious food in the world with complete abandon. It was tragically hilarious.

The next rehearsal was close to performance. I dressed the actors all in black, and had a tight spotlight come up on each as she spoke.

A lot of other work went on in between. They did their research, analyzed their script, worked with the thesaurus, did it in gibberish, used a three-way mirror, and much more. But the smashing success of the show came from the experimentation with the settings. The awareness that grew out of that work would never have been there if we had rehearsed it in a straightforward manner.

Note: *Eating Out* is from a collection called *Ten-Minute Plays* from The Actors Theater of Louisville. There is also *More Ten-Minute Plays* from The Actors Theater. My beginning classes do two character scenes. My advanced classes do ensemble work using three to five characters. The collections above are very rich with material that teachers and students should find exciting.

Some of the Tape Technique variations that follow will be very useful at this rehearsal.

Using The Tape Technique in a Confined Space

If I could, my first rehearsal would be fully propped and costumed, with a floating set, one that could easily change if actors found certain movements more comfortable. But there is an exercise using the Tape Technique that will help actors tune to the Repels-Impels-Compels.

After the actors have gone through the scene with the Tape Technique a few times, have them retape. While they are gone, use tape or chalk to create a small circle, about the size of a small elevator, on the floor. Put the actors inside the circle—no props, no chairs, nothing. They are to respond to the Repels-Impels-Compels as best they can. They can turn their back, move to the far edge of the circle, get in each other's faces. They can't leave the circle. Remind them to ask, "How do I feel when I say that?" "How do I feel when I hear that?" Let the emotion move you. You can make the circle bigger or smaller. This tight proximity should magnify the impulses, and make it easier to notice when they fail to take them.

Once again I would caution the director not to point out when the actor didn't take a Repel-Impel-Compel. Try to lead them to that awareness by asking them about the moment or beat when they felt they were negating the impulse. Ask questions like, "What did you feel when you said that line?" If they don't remember, they don't. You don't want to tell them that they were obviously repelled, because the next time they might be impelled or compelled. It's a sorting out process.

Recording Other Actors

Through arrogance, laziness or just exhausted imagination, an actor may feel he or she has found the key to a part. The actor then settles into some choices that could be improved on or investigated more. Sometimes, for whatever reason, the work has stalled. A little shock treatment, however, will jump-start the imagination and get the work going forward again. One way to do that is to find some different actors (preferably ones who have not seen your original cast do the scene) and have them tape the scene their way. Then direct the original actors to act the scene out to this new vocal interpretation.

We all have our own rhythms, tempos, ways of stressing certain words, and ways of doing things. When it comes to actors doing characters, the same principle applies. Each actor has a unique way of interpreting a part. That's why one actor gets cast and another one doesn't. That's the idea behind this exercise. The actors who tape the scene cold are going to bring some different ideas to their parts. These aren't right/wrong or better/worse. They're just different.

The purpose here is for the original actors to leave themselves open. They shouldn't try to force new ideas into what they've been doing. They shouldn't anticipate; they should just go with whatever comes off the tape. If all of a sudden there is a laugh at the place they were so serious before, let it go. Play the laugh, see where it takes them. This is fun and usually injects something fresh into the scene the next time it's played.

Watching Other Actors Act It Out

This exercise is the same idea as having other actors tape the scene and the original actors play it out. The difference here is that the actors see that other physical choices are possible. A director can talk about this forever and really not get anywhere short of making a beanbag out of the actor, saying things like, "Sit on that line," "Throw the pillow when he says that." That dictator/director is what this work is trying to get away from.

Just by seeing other actors make other physical choices, the doors of the imagination are blown open. The worst thing that can happen is that you steal a good move, the best is, you come up with a new idea that has more impact.

Changing Parts

This exercise is fun and can lead to some very interesting ideas. Don't try this until the actors are comfortable with their parts. They are digging in and getting some nice moments. Have them switch parts for one taping, then come back and act it out.

Note: No gender bending here. If men and women are exchanging parts, change the lines accordingly. For example, if the line mentions "your pantyhose," change it to "your boxer shorts."

A couple of things happen here. For one, every actor wishes his or her partner would do a line or action in a certain way. This lets the actor get that out without upsetting the other actor. It also does much more. This exercise creates an empathy between the characters by getting them inside each other's skin. It also creates a stronger working bond between the actors by making them familiar with the creative and technical problems that each is trying to solve.

Note: On more than one occasion, this exercise has led to the mutual discovery that each actor was more comfortable in, and able to bring more to, the other actor's part. When we all saw that, we flip-flopped parts and got a better show for it.

Chapter Four

Audition and Rehearsal Applications of the Whelan Tape Technique

COMMERCIAL AUDITIONS

I did a seminar in Miami. One of those attending was a casting agent. I demonstrated my technique for commercial auditions. A week later, I ran into the agent at a night club. He told me his agency had cast a few commercials that week and "every actor in Miami came in with a mini-cassette using your technique." Mini-cassettes and earplugs are inexpensive. They are worth whatever an actor can afford, as you will see.

This technique is so simple that at seminars I do it first, then ask for two volunteers. I give each a piece of commercial copy and have them read it into the mini-cassette recorder. The only thing I tell them is to read it much more slowly than normal. Then I put the earplug in their ear, take the script out of their hand, put the mini in their pocket, turn on the cassette, and say go. I pick a spot on the wall and tell them that's the camera.

They hear their voice on tape, and repeat the words out loud. The worst of them are almost perfect. They are shocked. "I did that!" The mechanics are so simple anybody can work it out in five minutes. Most of you have been unwittingly practicing this skill for awhile. Didn't you ever sing along with your Walkman? The advantages to the actor and casting people should be obvious.

Advantages for actors:

1. You are looking into the camera 100 percent of the time, not bobbing up and down looking for lines on a script.
2. You are not burning a lot of energy in the mechanical process of holding a script, finding where you are, trying to remember the words, or reading. All that energy is free to go into your characterization.
3. The momentum of your characterization is not disrupted by breaking concentration every few seconds to look down at the page.
4. Your hands are free to hold products or use gestures that add interest to what you are doing.
5. You are way ahead of others auditioning because the producer saw 30 to 50 percent more of you.

The casting people and producer get to see what the actor can do. They see things they can't usually see when actors' heads move up and down to read the script. Sometimes the actor's face is in the script so much that I think she is selling hair products, because all you see is hair. She may be doing great stuff with her face, but producers never see it. Eventually, this is the way it will be done in the future. Mr. Producer, you can make sure you see the actors at their best by having a mini-cassette recorder and a few cheap single earplugs at the audition.

I know about idiot (cue) cards, but of the thousands of commercials that are cast, only a small percentage use them, especially outside of major markets. Script in hand still dominates. The Tape Technique is superior to cue cards. When the lines are inside you, you are not forced to mechanically read, which burns energy and distracts you by obligating you to go to a specific camera position to find the words. This limits the angles and looks you can give.

DRAMATIC AUDITIONS

Many times when you go to audition for a play or film, they will give you a monologue from the script. You can have the same advantage here as you do in the commercial audition. Actually, your advantage is bigger in this case, because most theater and films demand more from an actor than does a shaving cream or chewing gum commercial. You have the freedom to use your eyes and hands and to express your dramatic or comedic talent. This gives you creative powers you never felt while doing a script-in-hand audition.

I dropped by one of the better theaters in Miami Beach one day. A producer and director were waiting for an actress to audition. I had been telling them about the technique. The audition piece was a long monologue. I said, "Hey, you want to try something interesting? Let the actress use the technique." They said if she wanted to, okay. The actress came in. I explained the technique to her and asked if she wanted to try it. She agreed.

The actress and I went back to the dressing room where she read the script once to get the sense of it. Then we recorded this rambling, two-page monologue. We came out, she climbed onto the stage, put the earplug in, and ripped into that monologue. She ate it alive, moving all over the stage with the momentum of the speech growing from beginning to end. When she finished, everybody said "wow," and she had the part.

The actress was very excited, and so was I. She came off the street cold. I explained a way of working that she had never heard of, but she had mastered the technique in five minutes.

REHEARSAL USING TWO MINI-CASSETTE RECORDERS

This is an interesting variation using two mini-cassette recorders, each with a single earplug.

The actors tape the scene as if they were doing the normal Tape Technique, except they use both recorders. They tape the scene, and then rewind both recorders. Using the single earplug, they act out the scene. By putting the small recorders in their pockets, they have their hands free. Now they hear all the lines inside their heads. One actor hears his recorded line, and then vocalizes it. The other actor also hears it on tape, and then she hears her partner's live voice. She then hears her own recorded line and vocalizes it.

The actors' responses are rich with the feeling generated by the emotional content of the line they heard and the line they said. They have the place, the props and the Repels-Impels-Compels, but they add the dimension of the live voice.

In my class at Orlando College we ran a four-person scene this way, but that's as far as I've taken it. I suppose a cast of ten could pull this off with some work.

This variation should be worked after the Whelan Tape Technique has been run normally for awhile. One of the major advantages of the Tape Technique is removing all the actors' obligations, except staying in contact with the other actors and their own emotions. The obligation to remember what they just heard and to find the proper emotional tone to vocalize the line would negate that advantage.

This application offers many benefits to the actor, but it's also just plain fun. Two or three actors can grab any script and do it instantly. Don't forget how valuable the pause button can be. The only rule—as in all acting—is not to break character for any reason.

Two of my students were doing this variation the other day in L.A. One actor had a hole in his pocket, and the recorder slipped into his pant leg. It was great. He calmly unplugged his earphone, fished around in his pant cuff until he pulled out the recorder, plugged in his ear piece, rewound the tape to the right place, and, having never left character, continued. The other actor never left character either. In fact, he came up with some very interesting business, while his partner made the necessary technical adjustment.

Note: No actor who has worked the Pause Technique will ever be thrown if a cue doesn't come "on time."

USING THE TAPE TECHNIQUE IN LATER REHEARSALS

Although the Tape Technique is primarily for work in the first half of rehearsal, it is also useful after the actors have learned their lines, done their research, analyzed the script, and added all the props and costumes. The set is in place and dressed. At this point do one more taping, and let the actors go through the technique one more time. Not having to verbalize the lines frees enough energy so some last-minute refinements are possible. Sometimes new business comes out of this. Occasionally an important moment that has been overlooked comes to light. It's also interesting to see the difference between that first tentative tape session, and this, the almost-ready-to-open production.

CLASSWORK USING ONE MINI-CASSETTE RECORDER

I once had a student whose acting partner got called out of town the night of a showcase. It looked like weeks of work was down the drain. Ordinarily in a situation like this, another actor would have gone on with him "on book"—that is, carrying a script and reading from it, which gives the other actor very little to work with. Instead of doing this, I decided to tape the scene with him, explaining to the audience what we were going to do.

We hit the dressing room, taped the scene, and I went on stage with him. I could hear him on tape on the earphone of the cassette recorder I carried, and then out loud in my other ear. I could hear my line, and then deliver it to him. Because the mini-cassette was in my pocket, I had both hands free. I could make eye contact all the way. When he went slower than our original recording, I simply slipped my hand into my pocket, and hit the pause button, waiting for him to catch up. I filled the space, dealing with objects, moved by my emotions from the previous lines. It went perfectly.

Note: The timing on this is easy to pick up. Try it once and you will see this is true. Going on with "book" never worked nearly as well.

I have also used this variation when someone's partner failed to show up for class. It's one thing to miss the experience because the work that night didn't leave time, but to miss just because your partner wasn't there is bad news. Ask any actor who has gone through it. It's a good idea to work with someone else at some point anyhow. You get different responses, and that makes you take a fresh look at what you've been doing. With this technique you can rehearse when your partner isn't available. Your roommate or friend can fill in. That person doesn't have to memorize the scene, but you're still getting nice, clean cues, eye contact, the whole deal.

USING THE TAPE TECHNIQUE AND THE STAGED READING

Staged readings – sometimes called a backer's audition – is when a playwright or producer gets some actors together to read a play or movie script. Business people come to check out the show as a possible investment, or writers might want to see how it looks and sounds for their own reasons. Before the Tape Technique existed, actors sat around and read the script to an audience. They got up, scripts in hand, and tried to give the thing some life by moving around. If there's something more distracting than watching an actor fill in for a missing performer with a script in hand, it's watching a bunch of actors trying to move through a whole play in this awkward fashion.

I don't think you have to be a show biz genius to see how much more the backer or playwright could get out of this ritual if all the actors were without scripts, looking at each other, handling props with ease, making physical contact, and achieving all the other advantages that are part of the Whelan Tape Technique. So forget staged readings. This technique is obviously a better way. Let the tape do it.

I was hired to direct a reading of a new play. I didn't tell the producer or the playwright that I was going to use the technique. None had ever seen it. I explained it to the actors after I had taped their traditional reading. The producer and playwright were appreciatively stunned by how much more they saw, and the actors were awed by their own performances. I loved it.

USING THE TAPE TECHNIQUE WITH KIDS

The Tape Technique works great with kids. The best part is that they are not bound up by having to change from the way they were trained.

When I work with kids, I don't do fluff. My classes are for professionals. They will be asked to do difficult parts. So the material I work on with the kids is demanding, but nothing they haven't already seen on an after-school special or in real life. We do drama – scenes about drugs, sexual abuse, being orphaned. It's not all doom and gloom though. Comedy is welcome. Finding good material for young actors is tough enough; finding good comedy is almost impossible, but we look.

I had a class with some kids who couldn't read. So I picked a kid just old enough to read and had him do the taping for the nonreaders. Just because the other kids couldn't read did not mean they couldn't understand concepts like death of a parent. Using the Whelan Tape Technique, they memorized complex dramatic scenes rapidly. They also created some very interesting stage business. As with adults, the Pause Technique worked extremely well.

Teachers who work with kids are going to be thrilled with the results they get using the Whelan Tape Technique. Scene work that you might have stayed away from is a piece of cake. Your full-length productions are going to come together a lot more quickly and more smoothly. All the cautions about using the Tape Technique with adults apply to kids. Trust them, leave them alone, and let them find the character themselves. Actually they will respond more quickly and more fully than adults in many cases. Children have not been made insecure about their creative choices. When I do a kids' class, I tell them right away: "You're not kids in here, you're actors. You get paid the same as adults. You have the same responsibilities." Treat them as professionals.

A friend was going to teach her first kids' class and asked me for advice. Don't treat them like kids, don't ever condescend to them, I said. Respect their individuality and creativity. Just make sure they understand they are there to amuse the audience, not themselves.

Be a friend who knows the rules to a new exciting and wonderful game. Remember a time in your childhood when your friends were bored? Somebody, maybe you, said, "I know a new game." The first thing everybody wanted to know were the rules. So explain the rules and be thorough. You know what it was like when all of a sudden the kid whose game it was came up with a new rule. Lay it out for them nice and clean; they love to play.

Chapter Five

The Whelan Tape Technique Checklist Summary

GENERAL DO'S AND DON'TS FOR ACTORS AND DIRECTORS

1. DO set the schedule so that in first rehearsal you tape and run through twice for a full production and five times for a two-character, short scene.
2. DO have the whole cast there.
3. DO place tape recorder as close as possible to all actors.
4. DO put enough energy in your voices so that you can understand each other in playback from any part of the rehearsal space.
5. DO a sound and volume check after the first few lines to make sure you are recording properly.

6. DO create as much of the set as possible, complete with hand props.
7. DON'T pay any attention to stage directions written in your script unless they are given circumstances. *Black them out immediately.*
8. DON'T break during taping except at the end of a scene or act.
9. DON'T do more than one take each time you tape. If you get hung up in retaping a line or a speech, you're trying to perform, which is senseless at this point. It just wastes a lot of valuable time.
10. DON'T rush the reading while you're taping. Be emotionally correct, but don't rush.
11. DON'T ever use the same taping twice.
12. DON'T let them start without warming up.
13. DON'T ever stop the scene once you start to act it out to the tape.
14. DON'T stop for any long discussions between the tapings of acts or scenes.
15. DON'T move your lips when acting out.

DIRECTORS' DO'S

1. DO be satisfied with your minimal role at the beginning. You'll be challenged more than ever later.
2. DO make sure actors are aware of all major given circumstances.
3. DO tell actors not to memorize lines. Forbid it!
4. DO tell actors not to move their lips.
5. DO tell actors that their primary obligation is to stay in character. (If they do, the rest will solve itself.)
6. DO have the actors maintain contact throughout: eye contact, physical contact, contact through props (hand a drink, light a cigarette, take off clothes), contact with the environment (look out the window, examine a bookshelf, throw pebbles in the lake).
7. DO observe actors intently for lack of concentration. Side coach them back.

8. DO encourage the actors to Repel, Impel, Compel. Make sure they are clear on this concept.
9. DO encourage nonliteral choices in responding to the Repels-Impels-Compels.
10. DO tell them to forget everything they did during the taping. That's not the same as telling them not to *do* what they did. That's a different exercise and comes later.
11. DO make sure no one is resisting.
12. DO realize that the actors are in direct confrontation with the raw emotional power of the script after reading it only one time. Give them a chance to adjust.
13. DO take notes, but don't give them to the actors until later, much later. The actors will probably come up with something a lot better, and your notes may become obsolete.

DIRECTORS' DON'TS

1. DON'T worry about making the actors understand your vision of the piece. Try this once to see the value.
2. DON'T worry about asserting your authority.
3. DON'T let the actors work until you are sure they have all the important givens.
4. DON'T worry about the actors learning lines! Forbid it.
5. DON'T worry about blocking.
6. DON'T give the actors any business.
7. DON'T allow them to perform.
8. DON'T side coach any more than absolutely necessary.
9. DON'T put any obligation on the actors other than to look for and take the Repels-Impels-Compels.
10. DON'T let them get out of character. This is the only mistake they can make.
11. DON'T ever give specific directions or line readings.
12. DON'T allow the actors to overuse one prop. "Don't make a career out of the blanket."
13. DON'T expect too much on the first taping. Take what you get.
14. DON'T miss the importance of the Pause Technique.
15. DON'T be afraid to leave them on pause for two to five

minutes.

16. DON'T let them freeze or fall into waiting during the Pause Technique.
17. DON'T pause only at the big moments.
18. DON'T ask them to remember or repeat a particular piece of business, movement or line reading. (If you thought what they did was great, make a note of it. If they lose what they did and don't come up with something better, you can put it in later.)

ACTORS' DO'S

1. DO warm up your body and voice.
2. DO know all your major given circumstances.
3. DO maintain contact with your partners: eyes, hands, feet, props.
4. DO ask yourself, "How do I feel when I say that?" and "How do I feel when I hear that?" Let the emotion move you. Repel, Impel, Compel.
5. DO stay in character. Breaking this rule is the worst crime you can commit.
6. DO respond to your impulses, fully and completely.
7. DO stay in the moment.
8. DO take chances. Explore alternate physical expressions of emotion.
9. DO make hand and body gestures, and make vocal sounds without talking, such as laughing, crying, whistling, screaming. Just don't interfere with the lines on the tape.
10. DO trust the artist in you.
11. DO guard your concentration, especially during the Pause Technique.
12. DO make adjustments to side-coaching from your director without ever breaking concentration.

ACTORS' DON'TS

1. DON'T move your lips.
2. DON'T be afraid of all the freedom. Use it to explore the emotions.

3. DON'T negate impulses.
4. DON'T be literal in expressing Repels-Impels-Compels in early tapings.
5. DON'T put any obligation on yourself other than responding to the emotional stimulus of the script.
6. DON'T ever think about or try to memorize the lines!
7. DON'T think about blocking.
8. DON'T stop yourself from eating, drinking, smoking, doing anything else that would normally keep you from talking.
9. DON'T overuse a particular prop out of nervousness in confronting the emotions. "Don't make a career out of the blanket."
10. DON'T lose your concentration. This is especially hard during the Pause Technique. Your director might leave you there for a long time. Grab yourself by the throat and get back to the emotion.
11. DON'T remember what you did or said during the previous taping. Don't fall in love with a piece of business or a line reading early in the game. You will completely do yourself out of any chance to spontaneously find something better.

SECTION TWO

GENERAL TECHNIQUES FOR BETTER ACTING

Chapter Six

Class Work for Actors

No musician practices only once a week; no dancer, painter or any other artist works only one day a week. You may not be able to afford a teacher every day, but you should be acting every day. One way to do this is to get a group of actors together and meet at each other's apartments. Try out techniques that you learn in your different classes, or from reading or talking to other actors.

The first meeting of any class (or cast, for that matter) is a special case. The students haven't picked scenes yet so they can't use the Tape Technique. Yet it's important that people in the class bond. The ideas in this chapter will help teachers and directors get classes underway. They will also help actors improve their craft whether they are working alone or with other actors.

Any good teacher knows how important it is for a class to bond. I never let anyone observe a first class. If you're there, you work. Actually, I won't let anyone sit in on a class if even one student would be uncomfortable with this.

I use first classes to introduce many of the exercises that we will use throughout the course. I use many of the Viola Spolin Theater Games to loosen students up and get the creative juices going. A step-by-step first class would go like this:

The first few minutes are spent talking about each student's goal as an actor. We talk about the importance of professionalism and the creative and financial rewards an actor can hope and work for. Then everybody gets on their feet. Name Game is always the first exercise we do. It is physical and vocal and always fun. Everybody's involved.

Name Game

This is the first exercise I do with any cast or class. After five to ten minutes discussing the objectives of the class, everybody stands up. You should get in a big circle, giving yourselves some room. To get to know each other a little, you'll say your name as you move your body in a certain way. Then the rest of the class will say your name and move as you did.

I always start this exercise. I don't get too physical. I might jump into the air with my arms out on my first name, and pull my arms in and land as I say my last name. Then we all do that together. Everybody's in the air yelling my first name, with their arms out, and pulling the arms in as they shout my last name and hit ground. When it's working properly every foot hits the ground at the same time. We do that three times, and then I point to someone next to me to continue. Maybe her name is Renee Sucree, and maybe she doesn't shout, but has enough energy in her voice so that all can hear. While saying Renee, she moves a step forward and bows, and as she straightens up and steps back, she says Sucree. We all say her name, while mirroring her actions three times. Then the person next to Renee picks it up, and around we go till all have done it.

If this is a cast, they won't have a problem with the exercise, but if it's a new class and they just met each other, they may be nervous. Be gentle, but insist that each one takes a turn. You can learn much from the choices they make in this first exercise. Sometimes casts and classes are mixed ages. Certain sixty-year-olds aren't going to be able to do the split the seventeen-year-old dancer pulled out. Saying her first name as she went down, and her last as she gracefully glides back up. This is a great ice-breaker and warm-up.

A variation on Name Game is what I call Group Mirror with Sound. The setup on this is the same as with the Name Game, except any type of sound is substituted for names. This is a great warm-up for class or cast.

CONCENTRATION

Take a few minutes to stress the importance of concentration to your students or cast members. It should be obvious to them that if they lose their concentration on stage, they will have just destroyed the hard work of everybody involved with the show—their fellow actors, the lighting people, the wardrobe people, the ticket people, the ushers, the director, the producer, and the audience. They will shame themselves badly.

They should see that, but sometimes they don't understand how that applies to film when another take is possible. Explain to them that films, TV and commercials can cost $10,000 a minute or more. If they lose their concentration and force another take, they are wasting a lot of money. They will never be popular that way. In fact, if they get that reputation, they will be unemployed for a long, long time.

Basic Mirror Exercise

If you are unfamiliar with Mirror Exercises, see pages 11-12.

First, I like to work with fourteen students. If there aren't exactly fourteen, I will find a way to have even numbers. If there are fourteen, I will ask them to count from one to seven around the room. The ones with the same numbers pair up and spread around the room. Keep an eye out that the same people don't keep winding up together.

Before the actors begin the Mirror Exercise, I tell them I will call "change," and at that time the Mirror person becomes the leader. I explain that throughout the course I will give them instructions while they are working. They are never to look out or break concentration. They are simply to make whatever adjustment I ask for and continue. This side-coaching is something they have to get used to right from the beginning.

Once the actors start the exercise, I walk around the room checking them each for concentration. Some are weak. Some are strong. I will call "change" and check again. Some have better concentration when leading, others when following. Gradually I increase the speed of the changes until it's so fast they get lost, and just start following each other. Then I say, "Nobody lead, nobody follow. Just flow together, help each other, give and take." They will, for the most part, get in sync. An occasional comment, such as, "Work together, help each other, give and take," keeps it flowing. This is a good time for teachers to evaluate students individually. Don't worry if some have a real problem at first. Be patient. They will do fine.

After a while, I will say, "Cut. No talking. Please sit in a circle. Okay, does anybody want to talk about that?" The students who really got in sync will release the energy that came from their experience. Some can't wait their turn and begin talking to each other. I stop that immediately because I want it to be shared. I explain there is only one rule in this class, "Only one person at a time talks in here and only about the work we're doing. I will shut up at any time, but only one person talks at a time. Got that? Okay, you were saying. . . ."

Sometimes students don't talk at first, and you have to start the discussion. "Was it easier to lead or follow?"

Point around the circle until all answer. You will get a mix of responses. This is also a point of evaluation for the teacher, neither negative nor positive—just more insight into a particular student's personality.

The next question is, "Did any of you get in sync so that you didn't know who was leading and who was following?" Some got to that quickly and completely. Some got to it in places. A few didn't get it this time, but they will next time. Let them talk about that. It was exciting for them, and their enthusiasm will inspire the others to work harder.

As the discussion winds down, I come back with a speech explaining, "It felt good, right? Well, that's when acting is at its best . . . when you're flowing like that, not leading, not following, just flowing together. If you're up there just following or trying to lead the other actor, it can't be as smooth or as interesting. It's too one sided."

Gibberish Ball

Words are the frozen essence of the thoughts and feelings which prompted them.

Staying in the circle on the floor, we're going to invent our own language. It's called gibberish.

While studying at The Committee in San Francisco and later at Second City in Chicago, I learned the value of gibberish. Although that goes back to the early 1960s, I remember having trouble catching on. This is one of the most useful tools you have as a director, teacher or actor. I cannot overstress the value of this technique, and making sure your actors develop a facility with it will reap high rewards. Feeling comfortable with gibberish is hard enough, but at that time a simple technique wasn't being used to teach it.

A quick description is in order. Gibberish is a nonlanguage language. It is a verbal expression of raw emotion without the restriction of words. Since I'm going to give a step-by-step example, I won't say much more. Knowing its importance and the resistance some actors have to it, I set out to find a simple technique. What I came up with is what I call "Gibberish Ball." The cast or class sits on the floor in a circle with equal space between them.

This exercise has two problems to solve. First a beach ball is created from space. The ball, when thrown around the circle, must stay the same size, and take the appropriate time to get from one player to the next. Give one the space ball.

I tell them we're going to invent our own language called gibberish. Each of us will make up a word with a certain number of syllables. Whoever gets the ball will start their word with the next letter in the alphabet. The first player makes up a two-syllable word that starts with A, and then throws the "ball" to somebody else. The next player makes up a two-syllable word beginning with B. This continues all the way through the alphabet. For the second run-through the alphabet, use six syllables, then ten or twelve. I usually start the game by giving some examples.

A two-syllable gibberish word starting with A might be:
ABBA – AFMO – AKDI – ARSE
The following words could be: BAKO – BEFA – BOPA – BIFNE.
CALO – CEZOT – COCAL

Each syllable must be clearly pronounceable. The first letter of each word should be clear so that players can follow. Encourage imagination! Some actors will fall into patterns. ABSE, BESE, CASEY, DEPSE, EPSE, etc. Don't let them get away with that. When they get to longer "words," tell them to think of rhythms.

For eight syllables, think of a four-four rhythm:
AB RO TO FI / CA LA MA TU,
For ten syllables, think of a three-three-three-one beat:
RO LO TU / FO NA RA/ PI VO CA/ LAP
Or a four-four-two beat: DO LA MI PEC/ A QUI RAC ZU/ PO KI

You get the idea. At first they might count on their fingers. Discourage this, but don't break any knuckles over it. As they play with it, they loosen up, and the gibberish flows from their mouths. The first time I do this with a group, I might run them like this:

1st time – 2 syllables
2nd time – 4 syllables
3rd time – 8 syllables

Then I come back for a lightning fast four-syllable exercise. People crack up a lot doing this, and that's okay. Let them enjoy it, but keep it focused, just saying "No English" will get them back from making too many distracting remarks. When they mangle the ball, remind them concentration on the object is half the exercise. "What are you doing to that poor ball?" brings them back in line.

Keep track of the syllables. If the group is on twelve, and someone does eleven or thirteen, tell whomever they threw the ball to, to throw it back. Make them get it right. Enlist the actors to help in this to keep them honest. They get some fun out of busting each other, but stay on top of this, don't let it be an ego thing. There is no room for that anywhere, ever. After they go through the lightning fast round, have them get up. Depending on how many you are working with, split them into groups of ten, twelve or fourteen. Fewer than eight people can do this as one group. If there are two groups, distance them from each other to prevent distractions.

Let them have thirty seconds or so after that long exercise to say a few words in English. Then bring the group back into sharp focus: "No more English." Give them a topic for discussion. "Okay, now we're going to have a discussion in this new language of ours." The topics I pick are loaded: AIDS, nuclear weapons, euthanasia, abortion, something easy to get emotional about. With young children, use topics like year-round school, parents, divorce, the environment.

Some people have a hell of a time with gibberish, so be gentle. But don't let them off the hook. Others are great with the exercise. When you match up two groups, try to balance these two types. Get the discussion started. Play devil's advocate. Throw a few things at them to get them going. This gets very animated. Go between the groups. Sometimes they will cheat in English.

Note: This is very important! *They are not to translate word for word.*

They must tune to the emotion before the words fully form in their minds. Express the emotion with the gibberish. Don't let them use foreign dialects at this point. If you do, physical and cultural traits will dominate. Get them to work for "standard gibberish."

Go between the groups. Some will hang back, and others will dominate completely. Step in, and remind them it's a discussion and everybody has to talk. Sometimes you accomplish this by stepping into the group and asking a question in gibberish to the less active.

Sometimes a group will be very compatible on an issue. In this case, I'll plant an actor or two. That is, if the subject is a nuclear power plant being built in your neighborhood by the lowest bidder, I tell one actor he owns the land and will make millions. I tell another actor that she owns the firm contracted to build the plant. Such controversy spices up the discussion. Let them go like this for awhile, maybe five minutes, or more if they're cooking.

Then say "No English," and form one larger circle, and let them continue the discussion as a whole group. Sometimes they splinter into little groups, and then bring it back to a group discussion. I've seen a big circle wind up with everybody shouting in everybody's face. Now have each person summarize their position in gibberish to the whole group in about thirty seconds.

As we're doing gibberish, I tell them, "You might be wondering what this has to do with acting. Trust me on this one." It is one of the most important techniques I have used in my own work, and one that has allowed serious breakthroughs for my students for many years. It works!

After discussion, I ask if they were able to "understand" each other. There is always a degree of positive response to this question. It's then useful to point out that because the players did not have words to lean on, they focused on each other. Their concentration was very strong, and they communicated the emotional truth of their feelings on the subject. The actors learn that words aren't necessary to communicate the truth. And many times, the emotion underneath a line is the opposite of what is being said. Usually a simple question such as, "What happened to you while you were doing that?" will bring all those answers from them. However, it is best if they realize it for themselves first.

Gibberish Ball is part of every class I teach, and gibberish as a technique is used at many points during scene study and regular rehearsals. In scene study, I bring in gibberish after they have worked the Tape Technique for a few classes. They haven't got the lines 100 percent yet, but they are very familiar with the emotional flow of the scene, and they are pretty firm on the Beginning-Middle-End.

Have the actors do the scene in gibberish while doing a mirror exercise. Usually, I will have them do the scenes in gibberish during the third class. In productions, they usually do the play in gibberish during third rehearsal.

A story about gibberish. I was rehearsing an off-Broadway show. I wanted to use gibberish, but the actress working with me said, "Honey, I'm old school. If you want to do that go ahead, but I'm doing my part in English." I said fine. She did it in English, and I did it in gibberish. I exploded in places that I had been unable to reach. When we finished, she looked at me for a long time and said, "Show me how to do that."

If you don't use this technique in your classes and productions, you are cheating yourself and your actors of an extremely creative tool. Just because you know the words doesn't mean you can sing the song.

What's important is not necessarily the words, but the feeling underneath. Something else is just as important. I go back to Spolin to make this point. She has a game called How Old Am I? (See *Improvisation for the Theatre.*) This game is a great way to show the actors that it's not "what you do" that's important. The game has two parts. One lets them act, and the other has them concentrate. You will appreciate the results. Your actors will then understand when you tell them that acting isn't what you "say," and it isn't what you "do."

At a cast party in Philadelphia, after a showcase, some students told me they were playing forty-syllable Gibberish Ball at five in the morning. I was there till four. Considering their condition when I left, it must have been hilarious.

Bowling Ball

I picked this up at La Mama Theater in the 1970s. It works. Very early in a course or a production, before the actors have settled in, this exercise will establish the focus you want. Have them all stand bunched up like bowling pins, really packed in. Pick one person and have him face the others about eight feet away. Tell the group that on "action" you want them to move the single actor to them using willpower alone. The actor is told to move the entire group over to him by willpower alone. Tell them, if they can't see the camera, the camera can't see them—just a way of letting them know to keep eye contact. I like to stand off to the side a little, but near the large group.

Some points:

1. Watch to see they are not protecting themselves by body language, such as crossing their arms or legs. Tell them initially to drop their arms to their sides.
2. Nerves or lack of concentration may cause them to laugh or look around. Tell them if they were really trying, they wouldn't have enough energy to laugh.
3. Give the energy a chance to build, but occasionally urge them to double the intensity. Pull! Bring the person over.

From where I stand, I can feel the energy going back and forth. It's one of my first clues as to how good a class this will be. This exercise lasts about five to six minutes. Keep an eye on them. Make sure they are keeping eye contact and pumping out the energy. If it's a good group, you can definitely feel the energy. People may lean or sway forward some. As the intensity builds they may start to cross their arms, don't allow that. You'll see fist clenching, jaws locking. In ten years, I've seen only one actor get pulled over, but I saw a lot of leaning from both sides.

When you break them using "cut," there is a large release of energy. Before it dissipates, ask the actor who was alone whether he felt the energy. You will, I hope, get a big yes. Then ask the group. It will probably be unanimous. I inform those who haven't been on stage that this energy is multiplied many times during performance depending on the size of your audience. That audience will lift the performance way above anything the actors ever got in rehearsals. If they're well prepared, it can make them brilliant. If they're not, it will destroy them. The same rush comes from a camera, because when it's rolling what is photographed is eternal.

The immediate benefit of this exercise comes when I tell students that when someone else is working in class, give them that energy. You will want it when you're up there, so give it. I don't want to see students checking their scripts or staring out the window.

I said this earlier, but it's worth repeating. I have only one rule in my classes: Anybody can talk at any time but they have to talk about the work. Share it or stuff it. If words are coming out of your mouth in class or rehearsal, they better be loud enough for everybody to hear, and they better be about the work.

Usually this exercise is brought in as soon as possible in a new class, but it should be used at a meaningful point, such as the first time an actor is working and another actor is not paying full attention. Usually first classes are restless, so this happens as soon as one student goes alone on stage. That happens in about twenty minutes the way my first classes run. This is an object lesson that sets the tone in a positive way for weeks to come. That usually solves the problem.

The next thing I do is have everybody in the class get up and:

Tell a Joke

To make a point, and to loosen up a new class within the first hour, I have every student go in front of the class and tell a joke. Some will say, "I don't know any jokes." Tell them you don't care if it's the oldest joke in the world or the dumbest joke in the world. Just do it. If they still insist they don't know any, either you or somebody from the class should give them one.

It is always important in any exercise that everybody participates. It is the only way any real bonding occurs. If you don't use your authority, very gently in some cases, to bond them as a unit, they will never function as a unit. You will not have the best class you can. You owe them that.

I teach kids' classes, adult classes and mixed classes. Somebody will always say they have a joke that's a little off color. To avoid embarrassing the joke teller or the listeners, ask, "Will anybody in here be offended by a risqué joke?" Usually there's a little giggle, and people say go for it.

Now, how risqué is risqué? There's risqué, and then there is dirty. Sometimes somebody gets up there and starts telling a story, and just before the punch line, you think, "Oh no, they aren't going to say that." Actually, they just embarrass themselves more than you. Some will laugh loud, and some are embarrassed.

"Let's take it a little easy," I'll say. Usually they get the idea.

In classes with mixed ages I remind them there are children in here. When you get a kids' class, you might not be ready for some of the jokes they tell. It's like an improv, you can't regulate every word that comes out of their mouths.

One thing that helps is to make sure that some preliminary bonding takes place before you get to the jokes. Do this with group exercises. In my first class I talk for a while and usually ask the students, "Why did you take this class?" Finding a common goal is the first step to bonding. Some students are shy to reveal, in front of the class, the passion or desire they can tell you about in private. Draw them out. At the very least, everybody will agree that they want this to be the best class it can be. Usually, you will hear a deeper commitment to acting when the shy one hears the others open up and admit they really want to act or at least try hard. They open up. I encourage that by telling them, if they don't try hard, I'm throwing them out, and I already spent their money.

Realize that timid, little girl up there shaking in her boots, trying to tell a joke, has to be there, needs to be there. Why else would she do that to herself? Be firm, but gentle.

Anyhow, after the talk, we go to the Name Game, then Mirror Exercises and then Gibberish Ball with discussion. By the time they get to tell a joke, they have some sense of each other as individuals and as a group. This usually brings in a little self-censoring on the joke. Everybody loves a joke, we all know that. So when they're doing something people love, and something they think they are going to be liked for, they're generally relaxed. So they all get up, and they all tell a joke. You'll have some laughs.

Imitate a Friend

Have each student think about somebody who, at a party or just with some friends, they have imitated. They all know one. Have them come up and show you how they walk and how they talk. This is harder, but some are quick to get in the spirit. These things only have to go fifteen to thirty seconds. If somebody's on a roll and I'm laughing, I'll let it go longer.

You may have to really coax some people, but stay with it. Remember everybody has imitated someone else at some point.

After they have all had a turn, I tell them that the relaxed way they told the joke and the way they imitated their friend is all there is to acting. So tell them to relax. Don't let them describe the person with phrases like "then she goes," or "he always does this." Keep focus. Side coach, "Do them. Don't tell us about them. Be them, walk and talk like them."

EMOTION

Next we talk about emotion. Then pair them off and:

Love/Hate/You're Funny

As an introduction to the emotional exercises, I have them pair off. I tell them the only rule in this exercise is no touching. Start them a few feet from each other, but don't expect them to stay there. I set it up by giving them a three-word sentence. They are to use those three words only, saying them back and forth to each other. Those three words are "I hate you." Remember, they can't touch.

Let them run with this for a while. Walk around, and observe the emotional freedom of each actor. Some of them can't say "I hate you" without laughing. Some will spit fire at each other. After four or five minutes yell "cut." Don't allow any talking. Quickly tell them to change to "I love you." Let them know there are many kinds of love: brotherly love, physical love and so on. Once they begin, walk around again. Observe closely. Get to know the talent you're working with. After four or five minutes, tell them to change to "You're funny."

I usually precede this exercise with a few questions, such as "Okay, you're a kid, and you're walking in the mall. You see something you think is really funny. You start laughing your butt off. What do your parents say?" For the most part the students know the answer, and usually some start answering "Shut up," "Stop that," or "What's wrong with you?" Then I tell them to imagine they're in the mall, and their sister does something that really gets them angry. They get really mad and go off on her. "What do your parents say?" I ask. They respond with "Stop that," "What's wrong with you?" or "Shut up." Even if they don't have a sister or parents, they'll still know what I'm talking about.

From day one, your emotions have been getting stepped on. You're being "civilized." Your emotions have been pushed back. As actors we must be able to let the emotions fly.

If you think I'm kidding about getting more emotionally frozen as you grow, one Saturday I had a children's class and an adults' class back to back. The kids ate this exercise alive. The adults were stiffs, comparatively speaking. Considering this emotional suppression aspect of "growing up," actors have a lot of work to do to break out. We not only have to learn to be emotional again, we have to learn how to do it as somebody else. Some work is in order. The following exercise is very useful.

Emotion Exercise I

Emotions are to actors what colors are to painters. They are the tools we use to paint our stories. It doesn't matter what your emotions are. It only matters what your character's emotions are. So you have to know the names of emotions and what they mean.

As an exercise to expand emotional awareness, I have each student pick a different emotion. The homework is to go to the thesaurus and make a list, in ascending order of intensity, for that emotion. If there are words they don't know, they are instructed to look them up in the dictionary and write their definition next to them.

Next class, each student takes a turn. One at a time, they read their list in front of the class and then give the list to another student and return to the stage (if there is one). At that point, the student with the list reads the emotions, pausing a few seconds (beats) after each one. The student on stage has to respond instantly to the word with any physical motion that comes to mind. It does not matter what they do, as long as they try to demonstrate the emotion physically. They have only two or three seconds (beats) to do that, but make sure they make some attempt.

Go through the entire class like that. You can, if you want, stack the deck a bit in favor of the class. From Day 1, Exercise 1, you can tell who the more open types are. Pick one of them to start the exercise. Their wildness is usually a signal to the rest of the students to open up and go for it. I think the chance of that backfiring and intimidating the rest of the class is slight. After everyone has done this exercise, you can have the students trade their list of emotions so that in the end, every student has done every emotion. You should repeat this exercise, assigning new emotions, until they have run the gamut. Remember, you don't go into a paint store, walk up to the guy and say, "Gimme a can of blue."

Emotions are to actors what colors are to painters.

Here is something to think about in relation to that analogy. An article about color in *Cosmopolitan* reported that The American Color Association had released a catalog of 50,000 colors. I saw an ad for a color monitor for a computer that used up to 16.7 million colors. I would take that as a cue: You have work to do.

Note: Mel Gibson said when he did "Hamlet," he went to a dictionary of the period and looked up "melancholy."

Emotion Exercise II

Have a student take a thesaurus and write an emotion on the board. Underneath the word, have the student write fourteen synonyms. Have fourteen students each write one of those synonyms on an index card and look up the word in a good dictionary. They are to write one or two meanings of the word and a sentence using the word properly. They should then read these to the class. After that, put all the synonyms on the board and by consensus assign each a number signifying the intensity level of the emotion. Students can see that some of these differences are very subtle, but if there wasn't any difference, the word wouldn't exist. Subtlety is what makes good acting. Remember, anyone can get into an anger scene and scream for three minutes.

Chapter Seven

Choosing Workshop and Audition Scenes

One of the most important decisions you will make as an actor is how you want to present yourself in auditions. Every piece you work on is a potential audition piece. I would like you to consider a few things as you look for that next or, in some cases, first audition scene.

For those just beginning acting and for our purposes here, a scene is a short section of a script about three pages (three minutes) long, where two people are doing something in the same place. Hopefully, they are two interesting people in an interesting situation. This basic description will grow as you go. If you find one but it's too long, see page 99 for how to edit it.

Most class work and professional workshops use scene study as the framework for many investigations. Usually the scenes are taken from plays, and that's okay, but theatrical scripts depend heavily on words. In film and TV there is a dramatic/comedic tension that comes from the camera and the perspective it creates. The actor must create much more with silence. Many of the acting students I talk to have a real interest in acting for camera. The dialogue dependency that theater scripts require may not serve the actor, who wants to work for camera, film or TV script. You should make sure that you work with each as you train.

Two points to make here:

1. No actor who works for camera will ever know the danger and excitement that goes with working for a live audience. When all that energy hits you at the same time, it can lift an actor to levels that only those of us who have been there can talk about. If you're not prepared, however, it can destroy you.

2. No stage actor will ever know the thrill of knowing that when that camera goes on, your work is eternal. Don't think so? Watch Fred Astaire or Charlie Chaplin, or anybody who ever made you laugh or cry, who is no longer with us.

Why miss either experience? You have a right to both.

Whether you do a film scene or a scene from a play, one of the hardest things you're going to do is find a good scene. The easiest and best way to find the right scene for you is to go to the catalogs put out by the major publishers of plays and screenplays: Samuel French, Dramatist's Book Service, Applause, to name a few. The Samuel French catalog seems to have thousands. In this you will find a one-paragraph description of the situation, the characters and the plot. You'll know right away if you're in the right age range and if the idea hits you in the gut. If it does, unless the dialogue is hideous, you're on your way.

In my classes, scripts selected can't be more than five years old. The point here is not whether I am anti-classical. I have had a lot of fun doing classics and neoclassics. What I'm saying is pragmatic, down to earth. I certainly don't believe you should only act for money, but eating and paying the rent from acting is fun. Richard Burton, Peter O'Toole, Richard Harris and others have at one time or another slipped off to The Abbey in Dublin to do plays for virtually nothing. Many other stars return to the stage to refresh their talent.

Ninety percent of movie scripts, TV scripts and plays done in top professional theaters are new scripts. The characters in new plays are different. One big reason is that in *Death of a Salesman*, an excellent 1940s play by Arthur Miller, the central character, Willie Loman, never worried about his sons, Biff and Happy, getting AIDS. He was a traveling salesman, and he didn't worry about getting AIDS himself either. In *A Streetcar Named Desire*, Stanley Kawalski never had a nuclear nightmare or got soaked with acid rain. Lady Macbeth never wondered how much mercury was in her tuna fish sandwich.

People today do not have to consciously think of these things, they are just part of our everyday living. This is the most dangerous and exciting time in the history of the universe. Somewhere, somehow that excitement is in every script that is written today.

In 1939, the record speed for a lap at the Indy 500 car race was 130.067 miles per hour. In 1992 it was 232.482 miles per hour. The pace of all aspects of life is so much faster. Once again, that pace is reflected in scripts. Since you'll be auditioning and performing at that pace, you should train at that pace. The challenge this situation offers the actor is enormous. That is the challenge and excitement you want people to sense in your work.

Another thing to consider when shopping for a scene: Never do anything you saw some other actor do, not unless you're getting paid for it. As you pay your dues, you are going to get some really bad scripts to do. You must find a way to bring some flash, some style, something unique and original to that part. So when it comes to class work, pick fresh material that really excites your imagination. Remember, imagination is a muscle, you have to exercise it the same way a body builder exercises his muscles. The pace and pressure in new material is the best exercise.

If you pick something you have seen another actor do, your creativity will be circumscribed. You are going to do it the way they did it, or work to not do it the way they did it. Either way, you lose. I lost two students one time because I would not let them work on a scene from a movie they had seen. Trust me, you may do it better, but you are not doing your best. You are also not using your class time to best advantage. In audition situations, as soon as you set up a comparison with another actor, you have destroyed the opportunity to be one of a kind.

Prove this to yourself. Get a scene from a movie you and your partner never saw, and work on it. Put everything you've got into it. When it's ready, videotape it. Show it to your friends, teacher, whomever. Then you and your partner rent the movie. Did you do it better? You're glad you didn't see it first, right? Had you seen the movie first, there would have been less You in it.

SCENE LENGTH

You may have found, during your first rehearsal with a new scene, that it runs too long. Agents, casting agents, producers, and directors are professionals, and they don't need forever to see what you can do. In fact, they won't watch. Generally after three minutes they are gone. So your scene better be close to that time frame. Still, it has to be a hot three minutes. You've found the beginning, middle and end. Now you've got to get it into that three-minute format. You have to edit. Editing is an art, and the best have spent years learning how. Still, you have to do the best you can.

Editing

Why do actors have to know how to edit a script? Basically, actors in classes and workshops have to work on scenes that are limited in time. Three minutes is a decent average. Unfortunately, most writers aren't thinking about the problems of actors in training when they are writing plays or movies. So the actors must be able to cut a scene to get something good to work on and stay within the time constraints of the class or audition.

There are writers who write short scenes just for students, but part of learning acting is learning how to break down a full script to analyze it. These short scenes don't permit that opportunity. There are books full of scenes for students. There are two problems with these. Most scenes are old, and have been seen by casting directors repeatedly. I try not to let students do anything that is more than five years old. Don't tell me that writers aren't writing great stuff today, they are. You have to work harder to find it, but it's time well spent. The second problem is that the others are new, and have been seen by casting directors a million times. They call them scene books, because they have been seen—and seen and seen. Don't be lazy.

The competition is so tight that you want to do yourself every favor you can. Having a fresh piece of material is a big step in the right direction.

Okay, so you've got to edit. If you don't believe me yet, you'll come back to this later when you start looking for material. I find that when I tell new students to "just cut the scene," they come back quite perplexed often enough.

Remember to look for two interesting people in an interesting situation. When you find that, you're halfway there. Maybe you'll get lucky and find these two characters have a two-page scene and maybe another page or two. Nice and easy. Sometimes you can cut a third person from the scene, and still make the scene work. If you need to keep the lines from a character you cut, one of your other two characters can pick them up. Sometimes, you have to do some real cutting, and you might want some advice.

1. First of all make sure the scene has a beginning, middle and end. (That's called linear development.) Don't start or end the scene in a vacuum.

2. Keep the sense of your scene. Don't chop it up so much that it doesn't make any sense.

3. Look for lines that are redundant. Cut lines that repeat the same information as a previous line.

4. Look for lines that refer to past or future circumstances that are not important in understanding these two characters and what they are going through right now.

5. Look for long speeches that stop the flow of the scene. Many times such speeches contain redundant lines or unimportant details, as discussed in numbers 3 and 4 above.

6. Don't cut real meaty stuff. That sounds obvious, but I've seen actors take a real powerful line and cut it. Sometimes it was done because the line was inside a speech that wasn't vital. If the line's that good, use it by itself or stick it inside another speech.

7. Get a book on editing, such as one of Syd Field's scriptwriting books. It will help.

In regards to number 7, you will be asked to improvise as part of your audition, maybe many times. A basic knowledge of editing and scriptwriting will keep you from being redundant.

Redundancy is the primary fault of inexperienced improvisors. They keep repeating the same thing over and over, and the scene goes nowhere.

Running away from the story point is the second biggest fault of inexperienced improvisers. "This guy steps out of the alley and points this big gun right at my head. He reminded me of my brother, who just got accepted at MIT. He's going to study quantum. . . ." Forget about your brother—what happened to the guy with the gun? Stay with the story.

The Tape Technique can be helpful with editing, too, as I inadvertently found out one day in a Philadelphia workshop. The actors were working on a scene that had always been too long. I asked them to cut it on more than one occasion. They cut everything they could think of, and it was still four minutes too long. The showcase I do with every class was still down the road, but I had told the actors that I wanted the scenes down to three minutes. It was still too early in training to leave the Tape Technique behind, but these guys were desperate. I figured that might be the answer. I had them tape the scene once more, but when they came back, I told them to perform without the tape, just doing what they remembered. I wouldn't let anyone be on book.

They whined a while, but I pushed them, and they started the scene. They had been working with me long enough to know they had better stay in character, no matter what. They ran through the scene, and it worked great. I told them it was the best they had done that scene so far, and other members of the workshop agreed. They started laughing, and saying how they had dropped long sections of the script. I asked them where, and they outlined a few of the sections they had forgotten. So I said, obviously, since we all liked it, it works that way. It turned out that what they forgot made the scene close enough to three minutes, so I bought it. We had found our cuts. You might be saying, wait a minute, how did the tape help? They didn't use it. The answer is that having used it that far, they had penetrated the emotional core of the scene early. The good stuff stuck. The fluff fell off.

Note: Since it's easy to get caught up in character, you might not remember which sections you left out, so tape the run-through, then go back to check the tape against the script. In the end, just use your head. Your actor's sense will guide you.

Chapter Eight

Acting in Films and TV

The feature film presents some unique problems for rehearsals. If it's a big studio picture, you have stars flying in and out, actors are in for only a day or a week. The advantage to the small movie, with ensemble cast, is the same as for a stage production. Big picture, small picture, you're still going to have your key players doing small (two-shot) dynamic scenes.

I was hired as a dialogue coach on a feature film. It was a caper film with plenty of action and chase scenes, but the core of the film was the relationship between the two young leads. If I had been the director, I would have established their relationship so strongly by working on the intimate scenes, that the characters would be alive in every scene.

The Tape Technique Chopped Up

Films are shot out of sequence, but actors have to come up with the emotion on cue. Take a tape of the actors in the scene, and dub it over to another tape, only do it out of sequence. Put the middle in the front, the end in the middle, and the beginning at the end. Chop it up even more, just isolated beats. Play the tape and have the actors grab whatever emotion comes up. They have to access the emotion immediately, and do whatever physical action that flows from the emotion.

A twist on this would be to have two different actors tape the scene, randomly jumping around the script. Then have the original actors act the scene out.

Since we are talking about film, here are two quick lessons:

Garbo

A young actress was working with Greta Garbo, a famous actress of the 1940s. The novice noticed that before each take, Garbo would get alone, and do some sort of preparation. After a take, the young actress nervously approached the star. Apologetically, she asked Garbo what sort of preparation she was using. Was it sense memory, inner monologue, affective memory? Garbo looked at her and said, "No darling, I'm imagining my face 60 feet by 40 feet" (the size of a movie screen). Even with multiplex, and screens getting chopped down, that is still a very valuable lesson. Think about it. It's why many stage actors don't work in films.

As long as we're speaking of stars and movies, here is an exercise that can help your film career.

Star Exercise

Ask yourself:

1. Who, of the top stars, would I be competing against, if I were looking for roles right now? You're saying, yeah, like I'm really competing with Jodie Foster, right. Well, if Jodie is getting six million bucks, and you'll work for fifteen thousand, you bet you're competing with Jodie Foster—if you're a good actress.
2. Who is my favorite actor of my sex in all of history?

When answering question 1, be realistic. I would like to go for Robert Redford parts right now, but I don't look like that. Actors come in all shapes and sizes and some of the most respected would never be found on the "beautiful people" list. Be honest with yourself. You look like you look, and even if you're fat or ugly, you can still be a star. It's happened before, and you could be next. No matter what, you are doing what you love, and probably less than 5 percent of the world's population throughout history can say that. So do the best you can with what you've got, and sell it.

Now watch a movie starring your answers to questions 1 and 2. Watch the movies once purely for entertainment. Then watch them again, only this time never take your eyes off of that star. Even if they have their back to the camera, even if they are unconscious. If they are off camera, anticipate with every fiber of your being their entrance. Be ready for it, but use the time to imagine what their character is doing in the story during that time. Pay particular attention to their eyes.

I'm not doing this to encourage you to steal their moves, or become an imitation of them, cheap or otherwise. Although, if you're going to steal, steal from the best. The idea here is to attune you to whatever quality they have that made them a star. Hopefully, two parts of that will be dedication and concentration. Surely you will learn something.

SITCOMS AND SOAPS

The Tape Technique is perfect for sitcoms and soap operas. The stars of these shows have done their character work, and some did it years ago. All they really have to do is learn their lines and adjust to any guest stars or bit players who may be on that segment. Actually, the stars are so secure that it's really more a case of the guest stars and day players adjusting to them.

Blocking in TV is worked out in a rehearsal room with minimal props, much like theater, only much quicker. In many cases, the sets are so familiar they are like second homes to the actors. The advantage here is that besides helping cut line learning time in half, the blocking will loosen up. It's not all "directed." The actors are still going to have to hit their mark, but if that mark is in a place they naturally flowed to in rehearsal, it will be easier and look better.

Line learning has always been an individual thing. In TV the time factor is pushed to the extreme. Even under time constraints, the Tape Technique will be a big help. The interaction with the other players, without any obligation to remembering lines, will loosen everybody up and encourage the finding of new, more creative business.

Director Dependence

Probably the most shocking thing about film and TV to a theatrical actor is the actor/director relationship.

There is a quote from Treat Williams, an actor with a long and respected career. I've read it at seminars. "American directors are like fast food in this country. They'll say, 'Here's the shot we want to get. Here's what you're supposed to be acting like when you get there. Do it. I need hysteria here.' If you got the chops, you can do that," Williams says. "That's why young actors can explode on the scene, because they have some quality about them that's wonderful. But they don't have the technique. Five or six years go by and they disappear."

I found out about the actor/director relationship the hard way. After twelve years of New York City theater, I moved to Los Angeles and the first job I got was on a major, major soap opera. I had a speech of fifteen lines. (That's how you get paid in many cases, by the number of lines: 15 and under, 10 and under, 5 and under.) Anyhow, I had to play the president of a businessmen's luncheon club, for which I borrowed a suit from a friend. I was nervous since it was my first network shot. So we did the first rehearsal, and I didn't see a director. Second rehearsal, no director. Third rehearsal, somebody said "break for lunch," and I still hadn't seen a director.

I was getting into something of a panic. I'd never done TV. After lunch we came back for a dress rehearsal and then tape. I put on the suit. We did the dress rehearsal, and I still haven't seen the director. Now you have to understand that in New York your director is your mother, your brother, your lover, your friend. They'll do your laundry, if they have to. So here I was after years of that. I was about to go on, and I hadn't even met the director. So I was in full panic. We were on a break. Just before shooting I walked up to a guard in the hallways at NBC, "Do the directors ever give notes to the actors?" He said "Oh, yeah, they catch them in the hallways here. There he is." I looked down this long hallway and I saw this director talking to an actor. I beat it down there and waited for him to finish with this other actor. Finally he was done. "Excuse me sir," I said. "Do you have any notes for me?" The guy stepped back, looked me up and down and said, "No, the suit looks fine," and walked away.

Few directors in Los Angeles are known as "actors' directors." Realize that if you get hired, the director is not there to give acting lessons. TV and film are very technical mediums. They are always under pressure to get the job done. Time is very expensive. So you must be a pro. You must bring the character to them, and a nice, rich option in case they don't like the first one.

To do that you must have technique. Actors have tools just like carpenters, and we call them techniques. The Tape Technique will teach you to direct yourself.

Hot Splash

I starred in a feature (B flick) called *Hot Splash*, shot in Florida. I played a Mafioso. At one point my niece and her surfer boyfriend were escaping with my money and dope in a hot air balloon. I got the bright idea of grabbing onto a handle on the side of the gondola, riding up a little bit and then dropping off. The balloon was going to go over the ocean from the beach. So I suggested this idea to the director, who loved it.

My character was hiding from the cops and was disguised as a woman with a tacky dress, tacky wig and the tackiest green and orange boa. So I ran and grabbed onto the handle. The balloon started to rise, and I was in character screaming and yelling at them. The actor leaned over the rail and said, "Jeremy, you'd better let go." I looked down, and I was fifteen feet in the air, over about three feet of water. I waited for a wave, and timed my drop to catch it as it broke. It worked! I landed safely, getting tossed around by the wave as I shook my fist and cursed the escaping teens. I was dripping wet as I sloshed back up the beach to ask the director how he liked that little show. He looked at me and said,

DIRECTOR: That was good but next time go higher.
ME: Next time? Hey, Jim . . .
DIRECTOR: No, no, no. Listen, I'm gonna put Murph (the director of photography) right in the gondola, and you'll be in full face close up, all the way.
ME: Close up? Okay.

So this time the camera was three feet from my face. I was acting my tush off and so seduced by the camera that I was going higher and higher. I heard people yelling, "Let go, let go!" I looked down and I was twenty feet up and rising quickly. My arm was getting tired, so I waited for a wave and dropped again into three feet of water. Again my timing was good, and I landed okay. The shot looked great, but be careful of getting seduced by the close up—it can kill you.

A few other things that can happen on small, independent features: At one point we didn't get our checks, and nobody was sure if we would. We still had two weeks to shoot and I was out of money. The next day I was featured in a big scene by the pool of our motel. There were many extras and an extravagant lighting setup. Everybody was waiting for me. I stayed in my room. After a while the producer came in and said "Okay, we're ready for you." I wanted my money, but I didn't want to confront the producer. So I looked at the producer and said, "Jim, I've got a really bad headache." He just looked at me and said, "you bastard," and laughed. "Five hundred dollars would cure that headache, I'm sure," he said. "Well, a lot of it is stress related," I said. I quickly got my money, and the shot went on.

A funny story and an insight into the wonderful world of low-budget filmmaking happened when the guy we rented the camera from showed up at our location in Orlando. He started screaming about not getting paid and started toward the camera to take it back. The producer ran over and grabbed the camera, then they started chasing each other around the parking lot. The producer talked a mile a minute, while grips started throwing body blocks on the camera owner. I didn't hear what the producer said, but finally the guy who owned the camera calmed down, and we were able to shoot.

It's a kind of fun hell, working on movies like this, and they are in the casting papers every week. They usually treat you well during the shoot, because they need you in front of the camera. Just make sure, in case they go broke and abandon you on some island, that you have enough money to get home.

It's the minor league of filmmaking, but you have to learn your craft somewhere. Although it's not a perfect analogy, the office of Major League Baseball told me the average time players spend in the minor leagues, before they move up, is three to five years. A few did go right to the big leagues. Sandy Koufax, Dave Winfield and Jim Abbott are a few of the less than 1 percent who made that leap. If you're thinking, not me baby, I'm going right to the top, it could be true, especially if your uncle owns CBS. However, if you don't star in a forty-million-dollar film or a big Broadway show as soon as you decide that you're an actor, don't be disappointed. Take a look at the low-budget features being cast this week, and even if you would rather live on the street than be an extra, read the next section. You will find valuable information. To the wise, extras are actors who don't speak.

WORK AS AN EXTRA

It's ironic that the book with the most dynamic new techniques in acting in many years should have as one of its longest chapters, information on working as an extra. However, most of you will begin your acting careers as extras. If you have not learned yet that a good beginning is the best chance of a good ending, you will soon.

Let's say, and I recommend it, that you take a job as an extra just to find out what making a movie is all about. You know it's like having a license to spy. You can go almost anywhere on the set at any time. You can talk to top directors, and cinematographers, Academy Award winning designers, and many others. In other words, it's not only a free education, but you also get paid and fed.

Now let's say you're on this mega-million-dollar movie, and because you're young and stupid, you make a big mistake. Everybody hates you, and they all come up and scream in your face, "You'll never work in this town again." Then they throw you off the set. All because you didn't know a few little rules. Almost all of these rules apply to every acting situation. So, I'm going to set those rules down for you here and now. There are some other rules I won't get into, like don't hit on the star, but if you follow these rules, you should be able to get in, get an education and get out without making any enemies, and before they can type you as an extra.

At one time it was the kiss of death: "Once an extra, always an extra." It's still that way to a certain extent. However, I tell my students, two or three extra jobs won't kill them.

In Orlando, I got my whole class hired. TBS was shooting a bunch of promos at Universal Studios. I went with them the first day and taught a class right on the set during the downtime, which is usually considerable. The idea is, that if you're going to work in film or TV, you want to know what happens on a set. I got there first to see that they were fifteen minutes early, as I tell all my students to be in any professional situation.

The fifteen-minutes-early rule stems from the fact that earlier than that, they don't know what to do with you. If you're on time, they have already started to worry if you're going to show up. People who make people worry are unpopular. So fifteen minutes lets them relax. Also it lets you relax. Worrying about being on time does not put you in the right attitude. Get there extra earlier, and go to Denny's and have coffee till you're fifteen minutes early. Leave early enough so that if we get nuked, you can find a detour to the studio or location.

So anyhow, the production assistants (PAs) are herding extras into a big soundstage. My students ranged in age from 6 to 60, and there were about thirty altogether. I pulled them into a corner. They were about three weeks into a ten-week course.

They had been told how to conduct themselves as professionals and what to look for while on the set. It was a big call, about one hundred extras.

This was just a reminder. I told them:

1. If you wanted to go anywhere, check with the second assis-

tant director (AD) for permission, and if you asked for ten minutes, then precisely ten minutes later you should be standing in front of that AD, letting him or her know you were back.

2. Be careful not to distract anyone else from doing their job.

3. Get back in time from dinner or breaks.

4. Pay strict attention when being told what to do on "action," so you don't waste time asking somebody to repeat the directions.

5. If you are given a prop, remember who gave it to you, and return it when that shot is done.

6. Be courteous to everyone.

7. Respect any wardrobe you are given, and return it the same way you received it, usually on a hanger.

8. Sensitize yourself to the rhythm of the set. A good shoot is like a ballet: The flow is incredible.

9. Sensitize yourself to set etiquette. Watch how these professionals treat each other and how they respect each other. Rules 8 and 9 will let you know when it's okay to ask questions.

10. Most importantly, you're an actor. An extra is an actor without lines. Take whatever they give you, and create a character from that. Give yourself a very specific reason for being in that place at that time. All the rules of building a character apply.

The star might be acting his or her butt off, but if some extra can be seen picking their nose and looking into the camera, that star might find that Academy Award shot on the cutting room floor. Remember four Academy Awards were won by actors who never said a word. You are not just acting when you're talking. An extra is an actor who doesn't talk, and woe to the director who forgets that.

At the end of that little review, I said to my class, "You are representing yourselves here, but you're also representing me. If I get a complaint about any one of you, I am throwing you out of my class, and don't even think about a refund." This may sound like a pose, but it is very serious. I was able to get thirty people hired because a casting agent knew my reputation and expected that anybody I brought would be professional. If one of these people messed up, I wouldn't get another call, and all the students I could help after that would be damaged.

Note: Students be aware. Professionals thinking of hiring you often ask your teachers what they think of you. I know for a fact that certain students of mine missed national commercials and film jobs because I could not recommend them. I am a professional. My first obligation is to my fellow professionals and the good students who will come after you. Any good teacher feels the same way.

Warning: Treat your classes with respect.

Here are a few general tips for being an extra. Since I recommend you do this only three or four times, I'll just give you the basics.

1. Take comfortable shoes.
2. Take some sunscreen. Usually makeup has this, but just in case they don't you want to avoid getting fried.
3. Take a sweater in case you work late or get stuck in a place with a monster air conditioner.
4. Agents who book extras are everywhere, so it's no big deal getting hooked up with one. Florida passed a law that an agency could not charge an actor a fee to sign up. Too many crooks were coming into town, putting ads in papers, collecting forty-dollar sign-up fees from a few thousand people, and then disappearing. Many of them did that for months. They just kept signing actors up and never getting anybody a day's work. So check agents out with the Better Business Bureau, the union or some other actors. Do it before you give anybody any money!
5. Read the chapter in *The ABC's of Acting* called "A View From the Crew" so you know what job everybody on that set does, and what they expect from you. I've had students get upgraded (given lines) and they got S.A.G. cards, because they knew the vocabulary and the responsibilities of those on the set.
6. Realize that if your "call" (when you must be there) is six A.M., you will probably be there till six P.M. or later.
7. Unless something is threatening your life, don't complain. Do yourself a favor: keep some distance between you and the whiners. Most extra pools have a few whiners. They will still be extras when you're a star. You are only going to do this a few times so make every minute a learning experience.

8. When you get the call ask about:

- Location — get good directions
- Call time — when you should be there
- Wardrobe — bring some options
- The name of the person you report to
- Money — Don't be shy about this. You wouldn't take an office temp job without asking how much it pays.

9. Basically there are two types of roles for extras: upscale-money, yuppie professionals; downscale-poor, blue-collar workers and clerks.

10. A wardrobe is for actors and extras. Have one. Build it piece by piece, but look good. Have a tux, suit, evening dress. Have some sloppy things too!

Chapter Nine

Acting in Commercials

"If you want to be a real actor, you'll never do a commercial." I've gotten many eviction notices because I listened to that piece of advice.

Let's define "real," or "actor," or "professional." Some actors only do commercials. Some do it all. Some only do theater or films or TV. Who's a real actor? I have a place in my heart for the actor's saint who bleeds for his art and would never do a commercial. I lived it for many years, but most actors will jump at a commercial if it's attainable.

Let's say you get a call from your agent, or, if you don't have an agent, you dig it out of the trades (show biz magazines), or hear about it from a friend. Somehow you get an audition. Here is what you need to know.

1. If they want a farmer don't go in a three piece suit, with a British accent. Don't bring a cow or a chicken. Actually a chicken might work as long as you remove its vocal chords. But do dress the part.

2. There will be a sign-in sheet. Use it.

Typically you walk into the audition place, usually an office, and there will either be an assistant, who will give you "the copy" or the script, or it will be on the counter with the sign-in sheet. Sign in. If you know you're reading for "Bo," that's the copy you pick up.

3. Get the copy early.

Ask when you can get the copy. Sometimes you can get it a day before the audition, sometimes two hours before. You're way ahead of the actor who didn't get the copy in advance and who has only ten minutes to prepare. Remember there is a lot of money at stake.

4. Whoever is on that page, it's not you.

Now you will usually have five or ten minutes to look over the copy and familiarize yourself with this character. And it is a "character," just like in a play or a movie. In most cases, the character is eating something you wouldn't eat, drinking something you wouldn't drink, wearing something you wouldn't wear, or driving something you wouldn't drive. It's a character, so all the rules of acting apply.

First and foremost, consider the given circumstances. Is this character upscale or downscale, white collar/money or blue collar/working to get by? You can tell this very quickly by the way the character speaks, and by the product. Not too many Mercedes ads are aimed at downscale types. Those two givens tell you many things:

- Probable financial status
- Probable education
- Probable type of housing
- Probable type of job

Okay, so you've read it over a few times. You've got an idea as to the character type, and you've got a handle on the material.

5. When I say read it over, I mean read it aloud.

Find a bathroom, a doorway, anything to let you get away from the other actors if possible. You might come up with a very cute way of reading one of the lines, and the guy next to you could go in and use it first. The casting people will think you stole it from him. You must read it aloud. Certainly you've been in a situation where you knew exactly what you were going to say to someone and exactly how you were going to say it. You rehearsed it in your head over and over. You walked up to that person, your mouth opened and the words came out much different from what you had planned. Read it aloud!

6. Don't start your audition by fumbling around in your bag for a picture and resume.

You have a handle on the character. You have rehearsed it aloud, and you feel comfortable with the choices you made about how to say it. Bang! It's your turn to go in. If you didn't already give your picture and resume to the assistant, you have it in your hand, ready to present it. I say in your hand because you don't want to start your audition by stupidly fumbling around for a picture and resume.

This is a first read, so you will probably find only the casting director and a video camera waiting for you. The second you walk in that door, try to look confident. Nervous people make others uncomfortable. Always remember they want you to be good. They will be very happy if you solve their problem, which is finding the best person to do this spot.

7. Remember nobody cares about what they can do for you.

You're getting thrown out of your apartment, your car's being repossessed, and you haven't eaten in three days. "I really need this job." As a casting person, I don't care. Those are personal problems, and I don't want to know about them. If I don't cast this right, I might get kicked out of my apartment. All I want to know is whether you're the best person for the job. By the way, a casting agent doesn't usually cast. They look at many possible actors and select the best ones to present to the client and director. That's why the camera is there. But they are very important people in an actor's life. You might not get this job today, but two weeks or two months from now the casting agent may remember you and call you in for a part you will get.

8. Be at your lovable best: big smile, lots of energy, friendly and professional.

The first time you meet the casting agent is when you come through that door, so be at your best. They may spot something on your resume, a show they know or a teacher you worked with, and ask you about them. This could be a trick question. They may hate the teacher or director, so be honest but don't go overboard. They may ask a question as simple as, "What have you been doing lately?" Don't mistake this as an invitation to chat. Don't tell them about your restaurant job or the weekend in the Hamptons, unless you're a singing and dancing waitress or the weekend in the Hamptons was a two-day acting seminar. So you get all this preliminary talk out of the way. (All that took two minutes.)

9. Get on your mark.

Now you're asked to get on your mark (a piece of tape on the floor in front of the camera shaped like a cross). It's very important that you get on and stay on that mark while you're reading. That spot keeps you in the frame, in the light and in focus. So once you're on it, stay on it. Now comes a very big moment, the slate.

10. One cue or two cues.

The casting director will tell you if you are going to be given one or two cues. You may get two, one "action" cue to slate, and then another "action" cue to do the copy. If it's one cue, it means you slate, pause briefly and begin the copy.

Either way you do your slate, which simply means you look at the camera and say your name and agency and any other information they may ask for. Some will do a straight-on shot and then each profile. It's done in a few seconds but they may be the most important few seconds of your audition.

11. Squeeze all the charm, warmth and professionalism you've got into saying your name and agency.

Just as you first meet the casting director when you come through that door, the slate is the first time you meet the almighty client and director, the people who have the real power, the ones who decide who gets the job. If your slate is sloppy, lazy or unimpressive in any way, they will probably fast-forward right through your reading of the commercial. They may never see how cool or cute you were while reading. They go till they hit a good slate. You must bring energy to this part of the audition.

12. Ask the casting director if there is anything he or she wants to tell you about the character.

If you call a plumber, they don't ask you how to fix the problem, but they do ask what the problem is. If they say no, just go give it your best shot. If they give you something, use it. This is not a discussion. You're not doing Hamlet. If they say play him "real stupid," don't get into retarded versus intellectually challenged. Whatever stupid means to you, jump up and do it.

So you gave a brilliant slate, and now it's "copy time."

Hopefully, you are using the Tape Technique for commercials. You have your earplug in, and your hands are free to hold a product or to gesture. You're looking right into camera, and you shine. If you're not using the Tape Technique:

13. Memorize the first and last lines of the copy.

If for some reason you can't use the Tape Technique, you have to do it the old-fashioned way. This means that you memorize the first and last lines, so that the first thing they see is you, full face to camera, and the last thing they see is you, full face to camera.

14. The product is the hero.

Remember in a movie, TV show or play, you might be the hero, but in a commercial it's the product. Make sure you use proper emphasis whenever you say the product name.

15. The mikes on these things are almost always weak.

These tapes are done on less than broadcast-quality cameras, and the camera may be set 6 or 8 feet away from you. Put enough energy in your voice to carry.

16. Usually you are in a close-up or a tight to medium shot.

Don't bounce around. You'll bounce out of frame, focus and the light. That's three strikes and you're out.

17. There are three or more selling points in a commercial.

For example, a recent sock commercial mentioned color, feel and style. Each of these words has a different emotional appeal, and must be said with a different intonation, a different "color." Remember, emotions are to actors what colors are to painters.

18. Products are sold on an emotional basis, not on a practical basis.

I drink a certain beer, and this beautiful woman pulls up in a Corvette and off we go. What I'm saying is, you have to be as emotional about potato chips as you would be about winning the lottery.

19. The camera is your best friend.

If you're doing a product, like food, clothes, makeup, whatever, do it as if the camera were really your best friend. We all like to share new discoveries. If you find a great new restaurant or shoe store or movie or book, you can't wait to tell somebody. When you do, you describe it with great enthusiasm and many superlatives. The copy will supply the superlatives, but you had better supply the enthusiasm.

20. If you see a word in the text you don't understand, ask the director or casting director what it means.

Nobody cares if you have a vocabulary or not. I just want to know whether you can sell this soup. People who say words they don't know look stupid. And nobody's taking advice about what to buy from a stupid person. Ask somebody what the word means.

21. The casting agent might ask you to do it again, only changing it in some way.

This is a very good sign. It means they like you. The adjustment they give you can be something like be happier. It could be very general like giving it a different color. If they are specific, try to give it to them. If it is general, understand they like you, but they want something different. Change it any way you can think of, but do it much differently. Don't play it safe.

They may love what you did the first time, but they want to see if you take direction.

22. Wait for the "cut!"

Don't stop smiling, or whatever you're doing until you hear "cut," no matter how you feel about what you did. Don't make a stupid face, or say something stupid about what you just did. The camera is still rolling, and if you make that stupid face it will be the last thing they see of you. It might not have been as bad as you think, but if you tell them it was, they believe you.

23. Get out clean.

They saw you, and they talked to you. You got to read. Now when they say thank you, you say thank you, smile and get out the door. Don't apologize. Don't look for a compliment or try to drag it out in any way. Say thank you, smile and get out.

24. You are going to be on a stopwatch.

You may have taken your time with the audition, but when it comes time to shoot, you'll be on a stopwatch. The price for a one-minute commercial at the Superbowl is about $1,500,000. At that price, a fifteen-second spot is going to be 15 seconds—no more, no less. That's about $25,000 a second. Not many spots are that expensive, but every producer who is paying for one feels they are. It's your job to deliver the commercial that took you thirty seconds to read in the audition in fifteen seconds or seven and a half seconds.

Get a stopwatch, and practice hitting those spots in five, ten and fifteen seconds. It sounds hard and it is, but you don't get $10,000 or $25,000 for one day of easy work. So work for it.

25. You will be asked to do improvisation for an audition.

You must know how. The fact is that it is easy, especially in an audition situation. They will usually tell you who you are (your character type) and where you are (the physical place). This is very important, because once you know where you are, you will know all the objects that are in that place. That is the stuff that improvs are made of. You won't have real objects in an audition, so create them. But make them "real." Even one object helps, but if you're sloppy with it, you lose. They will also tell you what you're doing there. These are the Three Ws of Improv. Once you know that, the only important thing is that you immediately give your best shot. Don't get nervous. Don't stall or ask questions. Just do it.

Tip: Don't create other people in an improv unless you are directed to.

26. About the interview.

It might be short, it might be longer. They will want to know about you, your attitude, your personality. Generally, TV interviews will be longer than commercial interviews. Interviews for plays and movies will be longer than TV. In a play or movie they are going to spend more time with you on the job, and your temperament is apt to be tested by a more demanding work schedule.

27. Changing moods.

You've got to change moods fast. In drama, your emotions have time to build. In commercials, you're on the verge of suicide, somebody walks in and hands you some toilet bowl cleaner, and you're dancing on the tub. You have to do this instantly in an audition. They may ask for the opposite of what you had worked on and just given them. Have some set images that always produce a certain emotion strongly. Carry them in your mind like a deck of cards.

28. Do you have a boyfriend/girlfriend?

In classes if I'm not getting the right energy when a student says the product name, I'll get her in a tight close-up, and ask if she has a boyfriend. "Yes." I ask, "What's his name?" By the time that comes out, her face has been radiantly transformed and her eyes are shining. So that's what you say *inside*, while you're saying Coca-Cola on the *outside*.

29. Put objects toward the camera.

If you create objects, don't put them on the side or behind you, even if you're only using them for a second. You have very little time and you want to be in that camera every second. Desks, fridges, drawers—put everything toward the camera.

30. Enter from upstage.

If you walk into camera, try whenever possible to come face first.

31. Look through the camera. Don't look at it.

Send your energy through the lens, through the camera person's head and way beyond. Looking through the camera, not at it, is one of the first things a fashion model learns. It is important advice for actors doing commercials.

32. If you make a mistake, keep going.

If you're running in the Olympics and you stumble, you don't stop to make a stupid face or curse. You get right back into the race.

33. Use your angles.

Don't be obvious, but move your face around. Any fashion model knows it's not all big moves. A tiny move can change the way you look considerably.

34. Be sensitive to the product.

Create a warm, sporty, sexy mood.

35. Probably more than one person who makes over $100,000 a year wrote that script. Use it!

36. Watch commercials.

Click from commercial to commercial instead of show to show. Tape them, and study them. When most people watch TV and an ad comes on, they go to the kitchen or bathroom, they mute the sucker, or jump around channels. I want you to click from commercial to commercial. Study often.

Four Basic Kinds of Commercials

1. The Soft Sell. Think of someone trying to sell you a cemetery plot. They won't be screaming and yelling, hopping up and down, smashing caskets. The tone will be soft, low and respectful. Luxury cars, perfume, expensive clothes or watches—products trying to identify with class and power—will probably take the same low-key approach.

2. The Hard Sell. If you're from New York, think "Crazy Eddie." In Miami there was a car salesman who used to smash cars with a sledge hammer. These people usually scream things like, "No money down, no payments for six years, low financing, we're givin' them away, get over here now, do it, do it, do it."

3. The Spokesperson. Sometimes it's a celebrity, like Arnold Palmer for Pennzoil, or Karl Malden for American Express. Sometimes it's a "real person." That's in quotation marks, because the lady looking at you through the camera and saying "I'm a housewife just like you," is telling the truth. She has to be close, because there's a law about truth in advertising. What she's not telling you is that she spent five years training at the Royal Academy of Dramatic Arts, and six years on and off Broadway in New York City.

4. The Dramatic Spot. This is where you play an actual character. I did three of these for some condos in Palm Springs, California. I was "control," the head of the British Secret Service. I did some for Oregon Public Broadcasting. I was a Russian submarine commander.

Sometimes you don't say anything, but you still get paid as if you did. You're just driving "your" truck and smiling, or having a beer and smiling, or biting into a potato chip and smiling.

The question about commercials is, how much talent does it take to bite a cookie and smile, or shake your butt in a mob dance scene for some soda? Not much. Right? Anybody can do it, right? Wrong and right. You need three things to get a commercial:

- Professionalism
- Technique
- Luck

VOICE-OVERS

The four categories of commercials I named are not just on camera. Some people make tons of money doing voice-overs and radio spots. You never see them except at the bank. It's silly for anyone trying to make a living as an actor not to try to get a piece of this money pie.

To do this, you need a voice-over tape. With the state of high-tech home sound systems today, you can probably make it on your own or a friend's system. You can put music behind it, or other sound effects you think make it stronger. You can write the voice-over yourself, or take them off the radio or TV. If you choose the latter, don't copy anybody. If they want that particular voice, they'll get that person. Be original. Avoid taking your material from newspapers or magazines. Print ads are meant to be read. Take it from an ad meant to be said.

The tape should be short (ten minutes is long) and each voice you do should be short, 30 seconds is almost long. The people listening are professionals, and they can tell what you can do without listening to the Gutenburg Bible. Have one voice for each of the basic types. And if you have some characters you like to do, throw them in. Maybe you do a great surfer, nerd, snob, Martian, whatever.

In order to get this work, you're going to have to do a *cold reading*. Here are some tips for handling that.

Cold Readings

Using the Tape Technique with a mini-cassette (see page 6) is the best way to go when you have to do straight commercial copy or a monologue. However, if you have to do a two-character commercial, or read with another actor for film, TV or stage, you are going to have to read cold. It's ugly, but it's a fact of the actor's life.

The first thing you have to know is that you must make eye contact. You can't do that with your nose buried in a script. The second thing you have to know is that you can train your brain to lift whole sentences and more off a page at a glance.

Not everybody runs five miles a day. I certainly don't, but those who do aren't people who got up one morning and said I think I'll run five miles. They started with a quarter of a mile and built up over time to their desired distance.

So build yourself a file of scripts and commercial copy. Every day pick up a script and practice getting a whole thought, and then delivering that line to a very specific place. Build yourself a prop camera, or put a lens-high X on your wall. It's an everyday job. Don't worry about how fast you're going, just complete the task. If it takes you two minutes staring at the page, until you can look at your imaginary camera and say a complete sentence without breaking eye contact, don't worry. Just keep working on it.

You will get better. Your timing will improve, and within weeks you'll be much better. Not bad for getting a skill you will need for a lifetime. I'm not saying you will master this in a few weeks, but you will have improved enough so it will be obvious that with more work, you will master it.

You've practiced often by yourself and with friends. You can now snatch three- or four-line speeches off a page in seconds, and you make eye contact and emotional commitment all through the speech. So what else do you have to know?

Well, you should know that this skill must be constantly practiced if you are going to maintain it at peak efficiency. Now you're not doomed to a life of practice. That hard work you did should pay off in a job—a movie for ten weeks, or a play that runs for a while, or a TV show that goes on forever. Set a goal. Train yourself to get at least four lines consistently in the first thirty days. You will probably achieve that goal in two weeks. If you're in the business and "making the rounds," you will start to get jobs you would have missed without this skill.

Chapter Ten

Marketing and the Video Resume

Not everybody who takes an acting class is doing it because they hope to make a living at it. However it is an acting class and marketing is part of the actor's life. Every acting program in the world ought to have a section on marketing. No actor likes to think about selling. We want to create—that's our job. Somebody else is supposed to do the marketing. Time to wake up. That may happen later, but right now, ain't nobody but you. If you don't market yourself, nobody else will! I know you're a genius, you're brilliant. Nobody ever saw anybody as good as you. Guess what, they never will unless you find out something about marketing.

The minute you said, "I am an actor," you became self-employed. You are "The Company." You are the president, the secretary, sales, and advertising departments. Yes, you are the product, but you are also the janitor. Get a few good books on basic marketing. Find one written by some big time show biz public relations expert.

As long as you're reading, get a good book called something like, "How to Produce a Successful Movie," and make sure it was written by somebody who did it a few times.

All employees should know what the boss wants from them. When you understand what they need and all the things they have to know, you will get along with them better. They will appreciate your knowledge of their job, and that could translate into more and better parts. Think of it as a marketing skill.

VIDEO RESUME

Sooner or later, you are going to need a video resume. Ideally, a video resume is made up of clips from feature films you starred in, clips of you guest starring on prime time TV, national commercials you've done and the like. You don't have any of those, so what do you do? In the best of all worlds, you hire a professional to shoot a video for you. There are many who provide that service, but you can't afford that. So what do you do now?

There are two ways to look at this:

1. You make your own video, and it's good.
2. You make your own video, and it's bad.

Those of you who are going to send bad video are the same ones who are going to send a bad head shot. You're going to need help either way. Pay attention here to avoid embarrassing yourself later. Let's assume you are going to make a good video. What are the steps?

First you have to find someone to shoot it for you. Depending on your skills of persuasion, you might find a professional who, for whatever reason, decides to do it for you.

Second, maybe you find a talented video student who needs a project. Check the professional film and video schools, and then the universities that have film and video departments. Some high schools have state of the art equipment and solid teachers.

Third, if none of that worked, we are down to your friend who owns a camcorder. This can still work.

In the first two cases, you're covered, and you can start concentrating on what you're supposed to: the creative part of the game. If you have to go the third route, you're going to need help. Maybe you can at least hustle a professional make-up and hair person. If not, you're going to have to experiment with the make-up, because it's not the same as getting dressed up for a club. Guys, you're going to want a little make-up too. Getting all this done is possible, and it will surely be a great learning experience. Considering how important this video is to your career, it is worth the effort.

There are books in the library that cover what you need to know. They are written by professionals and provide step-by-step guides in all the areas you're going to have to deal with: lighting, framing, make-up, best color for costumes. Of course, my books can help you with the acting.

Let's leave the technical part and get to you. What are you going to do on this tape? You don't know? What do you do well? What you're going to do in this video is sell yourself.

Start with a short introduction. "Hi, my name is ______________, I'm _______ years old. I like to surf, play piano, sky dive. . . ." Or, you can come out dressed as Rambo and spit on the lens.

Let's say you do a high-energy, charming and witty introduction. What's next? Maybe you do a high-energy, witty and charming commercial, and then you do a heavy dramatic scene with a partner, and then you do a hilarious monologue, and wind up by singing and dancing to the latest MTV hit. Do all that in about ten minutes. Change your clothes and hair for each bit you do.

You will want to start out in close up, and end in close up, but make sure at some point that we see you in movement, full body. I don't care if you weigh 300 pounds. I want to see YOU. Speaking about that, this may be your only chance to cast yourself, so go for the gold.

Warning: If you're going to "break type," you better be really good. Overweight men who cast themselves as the hard-body tough guys aren't going to impress anybody. In fact, they will scare people. "Stay away from that man, he is definitely not in touch with reality."

Right now a producer could punch a button on his computer and run your video on his monitor from a thousand miles away. You could get cast in Paris from a tape stored in Boston. Got the idea? Get a good video resume.

Chapter Eleven

Actors' Notes

1. PHYSICAL AND VOCAL WARM-UP

If you don't have time for a warm-up, pack up and go home because you can't do your best without it. Every class, rehearsal or show should start with a physical and vocal warm-up. There are moments you can miss as an actor if you fail to warm up your "instrument" (voice and body). I have seen actors physically injured doing something that would have been easy had they warmed up. I teach a three-step warm-up that requires you to take an emotionally charged line from your script. Don't use "Hi, Marge" if "You cheated on me" is in there somewhere. After you have the line, follow this sequence:

1. Stretch and bend until you find a real point of tension. In

other words, when it hurts. Hold that position.
2. Release the line completely, pronouncing every word.
3. Release the tension.
4. Repeat the process, using the same line, over and over, sitting down, grabbing your toes, bending over grabbing your ankles, holding yourself in the up part of a push up.

- Find the tension.
- Release the line.
- Release the tension.

Do this until you have worked the whole body, and until you are really loose all over. This I guarantee: You will have connected with that line of dialogue on a deeper level than you ever imagined. Note that the line you use in warm-up may change from rehearsal to rehearsal.

If you are doing this properly, you can never say the line the same way twice. It will be impossible. The air is not going through your body the same way. The blood is moving differently. If you listen to yourself (or tape yourself to check later), and you are accenting the first word each time, or the line has the same rhythm, or is absolutely similar in any way, one of two things is happening:

1. You're cheating by not really working for and finding a true point of tension.

2. You have intellectually locked onto that particular read for the line, and you are forcing it, against the body, to come out the same way each time. Whichever the case, you're doing it wrong. Let go! Do the exercise the way it's meant to be done. Students, monitor yourselves. Teachers, help them.

Use tongue twisters as part of your physical and vocal warm up. Special attention must be paid to the tongue. It is very embarrassing when you're doing a speech and your tongue decides not to cooperate. There are more muscles in the face than in any other part of the body. "She sells seashells by the seashore" and "Peter Piper picked a peck of pickled peppers," as well as a few others, should be part of your warm-up. A bonus to such a warm-up is that it also alleviates the nervousness actors feel prior to a performance.

2. UPSTAGING

When you are reading with another actor, whether for a casting agent or for camera, you want to be seen. You've got to get your face out there. Just like stealing is good for baseball players, cheating is good for actors. Always use your eye that is farther from the camera or audience to look at your partner's eye that is closer to camera or audience.

Angle your shoulders so they form a kind of V with the wide part to the camera or audience. You and your partner should be about the same distance from the camera or audience. Don't let anybody place you in a position where they are farther away from the camera or audience than you—it's called upstaging. When you try to make eye contact, you are forced to turn your back on the camera or audience. They can't hire you if they can't see you.

Regarding this point, you don't have to look at someone every time you say something to them. Find the laugh, the moment of deep thought, or joy, or disgust that turns you away from the other person and in the direction of camera or audience.

The idea of upstaging is something every actor has to deal with. It is something you can't afford to have happen to you. You must know how to defend yourself against egotistical, greedy and stupid actors. They will try to get you in a position where they are the only ones who can be seen by the audience or camera. It is a trick as old as the trade.

The word *upstaging* comes from a period in acting when the stage was actually physically slanted, with the point farthest away from the audience actually higher than the part near the audience. An actor would position himself higher (upstage) than the other actors, thereby forcing the other actors to turn their backs on the audience to look at the actor upstage.

You can't always prevent someone from upstaging you, but sometimes you can. If I am working with an actor who pulls it on me, I first try to adjust my position so we are sharing the stage or camera. If the actor counters (changes position), I might try one more adjustment. This can get pretty funny watching two actors trying so hard to upstage each other, that they have worked their way to the back wall of the set.

If the other actor is determined, the only thing you can do is get physical. If the scene is friendly, I'll put my arm around the actor's shoulders and walk him into a position where we are sharing the stage. If the scene is adversarial, I'll just grab him and push, shove or throw him downstage of me. As long as you are in character, and your actions are consistent with the mood of the scene, nobody will get hurt. Once an actor knows that you're no rookie, and that he is not going to get away with that stuff, he'll probably respect you. After that, whether for the sake of a good show, or at least not wanting to chance looking bad, they will back off.

Note: When it comes to camera, another actor doesn't have to get you to turn very much to steal the angle.

3. GIVE WHAT YOU'VE GOT

I was walking by a theater one day and I saw a sign that said "Audition, second floor." So I followed the arrow. There was a sign-in sheet and a bunch of actors, so I asked "What's the show?" They told me, "It's *Watch on the Rhine*." I asked "Who's the director?" They pointed. I said, "Say, I want to audition, what part should I look at?" The director looked at me and said, "Teck—sides are over there." So I went and found the script. ("Sides" are what they call the scripts used to audition for a play or film. "Copy" is what they call scripts for commercials.)

Turns out, Teck is a Romanian count, and ex-ambassador to France. At that time I didn't even know where Romania was. I was pretty sure it was in Eastern Europe. I didn't think the writing was dialect, so I mixed up some Polish-Russian-Hungarian kind of accent, and gave it my best shot. I got the part.

The moral of this story is, if the part calls for an accent, don't go through a whole routine with anybody. Take anything you know about that accent, and go with it. You will be better off than those who don't try, and you may surprise yourself.

Something you should realize from this little story is that you might walk into a situation like this someday and have to pull out an accent. So play with accents now.

There are many dialect and accent tapes on the market. Almost every library will have at least one of them. Get them and put them in your Walkman or listen to them in your car.

Try playing with the accents when you go into a new restaurant or when you meet somebody new. It's very interesting to see how differently people relate to you.

4. THE THREE P'S OF PROFESSIONALISM

Finally, all actors must remember this critical advice, the three P's of Professionalism:

1. A professional is always Prompt.

This means you are fifteen minutes early for any professional engagement. That includes classes, rehearsals with classmates, anything that has to do with acting. One of my students lost a big commercial one time because I had to tell the producer he was late for class too often. Nobody wants anything to do with actors who are not in the habit of being prompt. It's thousands of dollars a minute, and forget you. The actor you're in class with could be on a set when the question comes up: "Hey, anybody know somebody who can do this part?" It's really not totally uncommon for something like that to happen. But you blew off a couple of rehearsals and were late. Even though you're perfect, and could do the part in your sleep, your name never comes up.

Warning: If you are around when this question comes up, don't recommend anybody unless you are 100 percent sure they are going to be a total pro and have the talent to pull off the part, because if they blow it, you might as well have blown it yourself.

2. A professional is Prepared.

This goes to the actress who told me, "Oh, it's only two lines." You don't get four lines until you get the two lines right.

I was auditioning in New York for a "straw hat" (summer stock) producer. I went in the rented audition room, he gave me the script and said, "Go to page 47 and read Bill." I had a way of working, so I asked him, "Could I take this outside and look at it for five minutes?" He said, "Sure, but don't look for anything underneath the line. There's nothing there." I thought that's why this guy's in the boonies doing dinner theater. For the actor, there had better be something underneath those lines.

When you get a job and you get that script, get to work, and don't stop till it's over. Exhaust every technique you ever learned. Put all the magic you can in those few lines.

At one time a kid could graduate from college and get on a pro-football team much easier than he could today. I might get an argument here, but I think if a great professional team from the 1950s were to play today's worst pro team, the 1950s team would get killed. I mean physically killed. The stretchers and ambulances would be quick steppin' all day. A lot has to do with money. Today's players are competing for salaries that in one year equal more than the best players of twenty years ago made in an entire career. The pride is not less, but just to play the game today, one must work a lot harder. A TV commercial featured a top baseball player pumping iron and saying, "There's no off season anymore."

These people train constantly. They know if they don't work hard, someone else will. The same goes for acting. While you're at the beach, the actor you're competing with is in class or working on the craft somehow. Again, one acting class a week is nothing. You have to work at it every day.

3. A professional is Personable.

Be likeable. There is a lot of pressure on everybody. If people like you, you will work again. If they don't, you won't. It would be a major career blunder to underestimate the importance of this third rule.

FIN

Well, that's it. I sincerely hope you get your star. Maybe you will, maybe you won't—but you are sure to have one hell of an interesting life.

INDEX